Helion & Company Limited
Unit 8 Amherst Business Centre
Budbrooke Road
Warwick
CV34 5WE
England
Tel. 01926 499 619
Email: info@helion.co.uk
Website: www.helion.co.uk
Twitter: @helionbooks
Visit our blog http://blog.helion.co.uk/

Cover image: Russian T-72B3 in the ruined city of Mariupol, April 2022. (Ilya Pitalev, Sputnik)

Designed and typeset by Mach 3 Solutions (www.mach3solutions.co.uk)
Cover design Paul Hewitt, Battlefield Design (www.battlefield-design.co.uk)

ISBN 978-1-804513-67-5

British Library Cataloguing-in-Publication Data
A catalogue record for this book is available from the British Library

We always welcome receiving book proposals from prospective authors.

CONTENTS

MAP OF EUROPE SINCE 1992

Note: In order to simplify the use of this book, all names, locations and geographic designations are as provided in *The Times World Atlas*, or other traditionally accepted major sources of reference, as of the time of described events.

ABBREVIATIONS

₽	ruble
4GTD	4th Guards Kantemirov Tank Division
AAMG	anti-aircraft machine gun
AFV	armoured fighting vehicle
APDS	armour-piercing, discarding sabot
APFSDS	armour-piercing, fin-stabilised, discarding sabot
APU	auxiliary power unit
AT	anti-tank
ATGM	anti-tank guided missile
AZ	*avtomat zaryazhaniya* (automatic loader)
BKP	*bortovie korobki peredach* (side gearbox)
BMP	*Boyevaya Mashina Pyekhoty* (infantry fighting vehicle)
BMS	battlefield management system
DNR	Donetsk People's Republic
ERA	explosive reactive armour
FCS	fire control system
GBTU	*Glavnoe bronetankovoe upravlenie* (Main AFV Directorate)
GLATGM	gun-launched ATGM
HEAT-FS	high explosive, anti-tank, fin-stabilised
HE-Frag	high explosive, fragmentation
HHA	high-hardness armour
hp	horsepower (metric) (0.735 kW)
hp/t	horsepower per tonne
IR	infrared
KhKBM	*Kharkovskoe konstruktorskoe byuro po mashinostroeniyu* (Kharkov Design Bureau for Machine Building)
LNR	Luhansk People's Republic
LOS	line-of-sight
MBT	main battle tank
MZ	*mekhanizm zaryazhaniya* (loading mechanism)
RHA	rolled homogeneous armour
SACLOS	semi-automatic command to line-of-sight
SNS	satellite navigation system
STB	armour grade fibreglass
UAS	uncrewed (or unmanned) aerial system, colloquially 'drone'
VSRF	*Vooruzheniye Sily Rossiyskoy Federatsii* (Russian Armed Forces)
ZSU	*Zbroyni Sili Ukrayni* (Armed Forces of Ukraine)

ACKNOWLEDGEMENTS

The author wishes to express his greatest thanks to Vasiliy Chobitok (owner of 'Armor.kiev.ua'), Alexey Khlopotov (a.k.a. 'Gur Khan', former owner of 'Gur Khan Attacks!'), Stefan Kotsch (owner of 'Kotsch88.de'), and Andrei Tarasenko (owner of 'BTVT') for their extremely valuable knowledge, discussions, resources, and information.

The author also wishes to thank 'Haiduk', the consultant on the Ukrainian forces for the game 'Combat Mission: Black Sea' on the Battlefront.com forum for pointing him to several useful Ukrainian sources, and the Ukrainian tanker known as 'Shawshank Redemption' on YouTube, whose videos are a valuable and rare glimpse into the Ukrainian tank force.

The author thanks Konstantin Popov (kpopov.ru), Lukáš Kaboň (lukaskabon.cz), and Maksim Prikhodko (techtraveling.ru) for generously allowing him to use their excellent photographs in this publication.

Finally, he also wishes to express his immense gratitude to Tom Cooper, for his encouragement and support in writing this book and getting it published, as well as to Dr. Alexander Clarke, for encouraging the author to start writing it in the first place.

AN INTRODUCTORY NOTE

The 'Main AFV Directorate' (*Glavnoe bronetankovoe upravlenie*, GBTU) was the primary body responsible for Soviet tank development and production. In addition to their military designations, all Soviet tanks were also assigned a numerical index by the GBTU, usually three digits. (e.g. T-64A was '434'), while the components designed for that tank would have indices that start with the tank's index, unless they were carried over from a previous vehicle (e.g. T-64A torsion bars have index 434.51.059). Factory indices were also retained for some Ukrainian post-Soviet tank projects, although these may have been abandoned more recently as part of Ukraine's decommunisation efforts, as there are no known factory indices for the latest Ukrainian tanks. The Ukrainian equivalent of the GBTU is the 'Central AFV Directorate' (*Tsentralnogo bronetankovogo upravlinniya*, TsBTU).

Many try to distinguish different models of Soviet tanks by the model's year of production (e.g. 'T-64 *obrazets* 1967 *goda*' — 'T-64 Model of the Year 1967'). In the author's opinion, this is somewhat futile, because it is not uncommon to see 'hybrids' between different production years as tanks are sent in for rebuilding, and the Soviets did not use such a system officially anyway. This book will not use it either.

Soviet tube artillery pieces, including tank guns, also had two different designation systems: their factory code and their GRAU index assigned once they entered service. Systems introduced before 1956 are usually better known by their factory codes (e.g., the 100mm D-10T2S rifled gun on the T-55, which has the lesser-known pre-1956 GRAU index 53-PT-412D), while more modern systems are usually known by their GRAU indices instead (e.g. the 2A46, 2A46-1, 2A46-2, 2A46M, 2A46M-1, 2A46M-4, and 2A46M-5 125mm smoothbore tank guns; all have the same factory code D-81TM). The author will use factory codes for systems introduced before 1956, and GRAU indices for systems introduced after 1956 for consistency.

Soviet, Russian, and Ukrainian engines are rated in metric horsepower (1 hp = 0.735 kW). This is different to the imperial/mechanical horsepower commonly used in the US (1 hp = 0.745 kW).

INTRODUCTION

Russian T-72B in the ruined city of Mariupol, April 2022. (Ilya Pitalev, Sputnik)

The Russo–Ukrainian War, which began with the 2014 Russian annexation of Crimea and dramatically escalated when Russia launched a full-scale invasion of Ukraine on 24 February 2022, is the largest conventional war to occur in Europe since the Second World War ended in 1945. It also represents the largest use of armour on the European continent since 1945, for Russia and Ukraine possess the largest and second largest tank fleets in Europe, respectively.

The Soviets judged the 'technical level' or effectiveness of their tanks according to four criteria:

- Firepower: the ability to find and destroy targets on the battlefield.
- Protection: the ability to sustain damage without losing combat capability and protect the crew.
- Mobility: the ability to move to and on the battlefield.
- Reliability: the tank can be trusted to work when it is needed.

The first three criteria are well-known to any armour enthusiast and each tank's description in this book is formatted into three sections covering these criteria. In most books these qualities are usually boiled down to quantitative 'hard factors', such as armour penetration, armour thickness (or equivalent rolled homogenous armour (RHA) thickness for composite armour), power/weight ratio, and so on.[1] While these 'hard factors' are important and useful as points of comparison and for plugging into the Soviet mathematical models, they do not really capture a lot of equally (if not more) important 'soft factors'. These are much more difficult to quantify, such as the degree of automation, ergonomics, quality of communication and navigation systems, and cross-country capabilities.

In addition, at the end of each tank's description will be a 'Context' section that specifically talks about how the tank fits in within the context of the Russo–Ukrainian War. The author does not wish to pass judgement on any tank or say whether one is intrinsically superior to the other; rather it is his intention that the book presents the information and characteristics, both good and bad, of each tank, and the reader can use those to make up their own mind.

Due to the large number of models used by both sides, this mini-series consists of two parts. Part 1 focuses on legacy Soviet main battle tanks (MBTs), which still form the bulk of both the Russian and Ukrainian tank fleets, and post-Soviet Russian models currently in use in Ukraine. Part 2, published as Volume 5 of the *War in Ukraine* mini-series, describes Ukrainian post-1991 models, the organisation and training of both Russian and Ukrainian tank forces, and two battles where MBTs played a particularly important role.

1
A COMMON HERITAGE: SOVIET LEGACY TANKS IN RUSSIAN AND UKRAINIAN SERVICE

The 'three musketeers' of the 1980s Soviet tank force at KhBTZ (Kharkiv AFV Factory). From left to right, they are a T-72B, T-64B1V, and T-80BV. The T-64 is a test model that has been modified with the Buran night sight and no longer has an IR searchlight. (Vasiliy Chobitok)

It is impossible to talk about either Russia's or Ukraine's tank forces without discussing their progenitor: the Soviet Army's tank force. Throughout the Cold War, the Soviet Army had the largest tank force in the world, estimated at some 63,900 tanks by the Soviets as of 1 January 1990, *after* unilateral arms reduction measures had been initiated following the signing of the Conventional Forces in Europe (CFE) treaty in 1989. This was larger than the combined tank forces of all the countries in the world excluding the Warsaw Pact.[1]

There is no exact breakdown by type for the number of tanks in service with the Soviet Union. However, there are figures for the number of Soviet tanks present in Europe by type, provided by the Soviets themselves during negotiations for the CFE treaty for 1 January 1990. They were as follows:

T-64: 3,977[2]
T-72: 5,086[3]
T-80: 4,839[4]

All of these tank types are in use with both the Russian and Ukrainian armies in the current war. This chapter will cover the main models that were developed before 1991; post-1991 modernisations will be covered separately.

The design lineage of all post-Second World War Soviet tanks can be traced back to one man: Aleksandr Morozov. He became the head of the KB-520 tank 'design bureau' (*konstruktorskoe byuro*, KB) based in Kharkov (today Kharkiv), when Mikhail Koshkin, chief designer of the famous T-34 medium tank, died of pneumonia in 1940. As such, Morozov was responsible for the continued development of the T-34 throughout the 'Great Patriotic War', especially after the German invasion forced the evacuation of the tank factories in Ukraine to Nizhny Tagil, behind the Urals.

Morozov also led the design of the T-34's direct successor: the T-44 (Object 136) medium tank. While the T-44 was not built in large numbers and is fairly obscure in the West, its adoption of a torsion bar suspension as opposed to the T-34's outdated Christie spring suspension, a centrally mounted turret, and a transverse engine layout with planetary (epicyclic) gearbox transmission to minimise the length of the engine compartment would set the pattern for all following Soviet tanks. The T-44 can therefore be said to be the true ancestor of all Russian and Ukrainian MBTs, whereas the T-34 was really more of a developmental dead-end.

Aleksandr Aleksandrovich Morozov (1904–1979), probably the single most influential person in post-war Soviet tank design. (Morozov family archive)

T-44M at the *'Boevaya slava Urala'* museum. Though it did not arrive in time for the Second World War and was relatively quickly supplanted by the T-54, the T-44 set the basic layout for all following Soviet medium tanks and MBTs. (Konstantin Popov, kpopov.ru)

This new layout was perfected with the T-54 (Object 137) medium tank, the last tank Morozov designed as leader of KB-520. It combined a powerful 100mm D-10T rifled gun, ballistically well-shaped armour protection (up to 200mm thick), and good mobility, all in a 36 tonne package. Certainly, when the British examined a Soviet T-54A captured by Hungarian insurgents and driven onto the British Embassy's grounds in Budapest during the T-54's combat debut in the 1956 Hungarian Revolution, they were suitably impressed. As a result, the British would develop the excellent 105mm L7 rifled tank gun to counter the T-54.

After Morozov's departure in 1951, KB-520 remained responsible for implementing incremental improvements to the T-54 being developed by the new KB-60M bureau in Kharkov under Morozov, resulting in the T-55 (Object 155) of 1958. The T-55 featured minor improvements to the engine, fuel and ammunition stowage, and most importantly an NBC protection system for the anticipated future nuclear confrontation between the Warsaw Pact and NATO. However, in terms of firepower, mobility, and armour, it was virtually identical to the T-54.

The next-generation Soviet medium tank being developed by KB-60M, the Object 430, featured a new high-power 100mm D-54TS rifled gun. KB-520, now led by Leonid Kartsev, also offered the more conservative Object 165, using the same gun but based on a stretched T-55 chassis and hull mated to a new turret. The introduction of new Western NATO tanks with the L7 gun in the late 1950s, particularly the American M60, threatened to make the large Warsaw Pact tank force obsolete at one stroke, and forced the Soviets to seek an interim solution pending Morozov's next-generation tank. This would come from the KB-520 design bureau by modifying their Object 165 into the T-62 (Object 166) medium tank.

Meanwhile, KB-60M continued working on the Object 430; since it made no sense for the 'next-generation' tank to have a worse gun than the 'gap-filler' T-62, it was further developed into the Object 432, with a 115mm D-68T smoothbore gun similar to the T-62's gun but modified for separate-loading projectiles and fed by an autoloader. It was accepted for service in 1966 as the T-64 medium tank. The T-64 would receive several major upgrades, most notably a 125mm smoothbore main gun starting with the T-64A. The Soviets now had a tank with the firepower and frontal protection of a heavy tank, while still maintaining the mobility and flexibility of medium tanks. By 1976, the Soviets had abandoned the heavy/medium tank dichotomy and the improved T-64B was thus the first Soviet tank to officially enter service as a main battle tank (MBT).[5] It was also Morozov's last tank design to enter service, for he died in 1979.

During the latter half of the Cold War, the Soviet Union had three primary tank production factories and associated KBs based in three cities:

Disabled T-55A with roof cage armour somewhere in Ukraine, August 2023. This tank lacks the loader's DShK AAMG, suggesting it is a pre-1970 production tank. The roof cage armour has intercepted a modified PG-7VL projectile, likely from a UAS. (NMFTE Telegram)

Object 430, the predecessor of the T-64, at the Kubinka Tank Museum. Next to it is the Object 435, a '430' modified to take a 115mm main gun. (Konstantin Popov)

Russian late-1960s-production T-62 captured by the Ukrainians in Kherson in November 2022. Besides the roof cage armour it is virtually identical to Arab T-62s the Israelis faced during the 1973 Yom Kippur War. (ZSU)

- Kharkov: Malyshev Factory (*Kharkovskiy zavod transportnogo mashinostroeniya imeni V. A. Malysheva*, KhZTM) and the Kharkov Design Bureau for Machine Building (*Kharkovskoe konstruktorskoe byuro po mashinostroeniyu*, KhKBM; pre-1966, KB-60M).[6]
- Leningrad: Kirov Factory (*Leningradskiy Kirovskiy zavod*, LKZ) and the Special Design Bureau for Transport Engineering (*Spetsialnoe konstruktorskoe byuro transportnogo mashinostroenniya*, Spetsmash; pre-1991, KB-3).
- Nizhny Tagil: Uralvagonzavod (UVZ) and the Ural Design Bureau for Transport Engineering (*Uralskoe konstruktorskoe byuro transportnogo mashinostroeniya*, UKBTM; pre-1971, KB-520).

There was also a fourth tank production centre in Omsk (Omsktransmash) but it was mostly engaged in building MBT designs from other factories, particularly those of Leningrad.

It was originally intended that the T-64 would be produced by all factories, but for various reasons, the Soviet Army would end up with three very different MBTs with fairly similar capabilities. Both UVZ's T-72 and LKZ's T-80 started out as modifications of the T-64A in response to early difficulties experienced in service, particularly with the unconventional opposed-piston engine it used. However, in an example of 'feature creep', both ended up being radically different in terms of construction to the T-64A. This wasted a lot of money, effort, and most importantly, time: it allowed the West to catch-up and leapfrog the Soviets with their own next-generation of tanks like the M1 Abrams and Leopard 2. The decision to produce three tanks concurrently has been called a 'crime against the state' by Soviet armour historians Andrei Tarasenko and Vsevolod Chernyshev.[7]

The T-64, T-72, and T-80 each have their own proponents and detractors, leading to a lot of heated arguments by enthusiasts over which was the 'superior' tank. This is also not helped by the fact that the T-64's primary user is Ukraine, while Russia uses the T-72 and T-80, and such debates will often get coloured by nationalism as well. The fact of the matter is that all of these tanks' origins date back over half a century, and the author opines that the Ukrainian tanker who goes by the name 'Shawshank Redemption' on YouTube (henceforth abbreviated 'SR') put it best: 'I just find it funny when they tell me one is worthy of its time for the 21st century and the other is outdated, even though in fact all are outdated. It's obvious.'

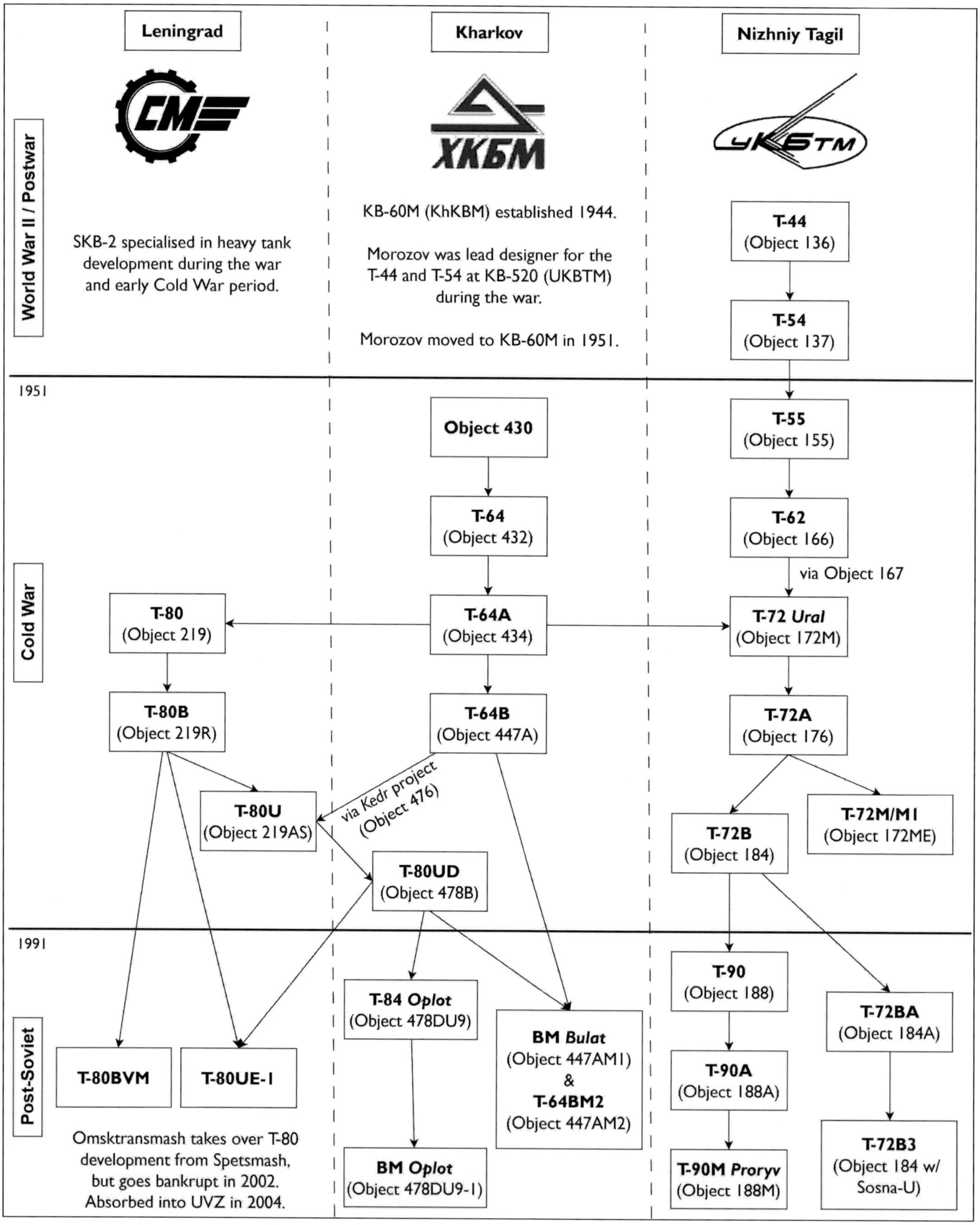

Genealogy of Soviet, Russian, and Ukrainian medium and main battle tanks, arranged in roughly chronological order. For lack of space, not all models are shown. Logos are trademarks of their respective design bureaus.

1.1: T-64: Morozov's Legacy

T-64BV of the 1st 'Siveria' Tank Brigade during tactical exercises in 2020. Note the small steel road wheels and the IR searchlight mounted on the left of the main gun. (ZSU)

When it comes to understanding the T-64, one has to always keep in mind that it is a product of the Khrushchev era. Nikita Khrushchev, who led the Soviet Union from 1953 to 1964, pursued a policy of reducing conventional force levels in the Soviet military and placing a greater emphasis on nuclear weapons. Among the victims of his policies was the Soviet heavy tank program. However, there is no evidence that Khrushchev himself directly imposed a weight limit on tanks: in its original 1961 requirement, the GBTU specifically stipulated that the tank's weight should not exceed 34 tonnes (later increased to 36 tonnes in 1966).[8] Almost all of the design decisions implemented in the T-64 were to make sure it did not cross this strict 'red line'. Although later variants of the T-64 inevitably became heavier, Morozov succeeded: the original T-64 weighed 36 tonnes.

Before the Russian invasion of Ukraine in 2022, the T-64 was a fairly obscure tank. Unlike its more illustrious and prolific cousin, the T-72, the T-64 was not exported in Soviet times, and it only saw combat briefly during the obscure 1992 Transnistrian War.[9] The T-64 was also not widely promoted in tank shows and expos, unlike the T-80. Very little has been published about the T-64 in English, and a lot of that is a mixture of outdated Cold War myths, half-truths, oversimplifications, and misunderstandings (sometimes outright misinformation by Morozov's enemies from Nizhny Tagil), resulting in what, in the author's opinion, is a somewhat unfairly negative picture of the T-64. This section will attempt to give a more balanced view and hopefully provide more detailed information on some of the T-64's unique design features than has previously been published in English.

There were essentially three 'generations' of the T-64 in Soviet production:

- T-64 (Object 432): original model with 115mm gun and TPD-43B coincidence rangefinder.
- T-64A (Object 434): introduced 125mm gun and TPD-2-49 coincidence rangefinder.[10]
- T-64B (Object 447A): introduced 1A33 *Ob* FCS and 9K112 *Kobra* GLATGM complex.

The T-64B was the primary model in service with the Armed Forces of Ukraine (*Zbroyni Sili Ukrayni*, ZSU) at the beginning of the 2022 Russian invasion, and this section will therefore focus on describing the Soviet-era T-64B and its variants. The T-64A is very similar to the T-64B, with the primary difference being that it uses an inferior fire control system (FCS). A few T-64As have been seen with the ZSU as well as with the so-called 'separatist' forces. The original T-64s were eventually rebuilt to T-64A standards (minus 125mm gun) as T-64Rs during overhauls in the 1970s, and are not known to be in service with either side at the time of writing. Ukrainian modernisations of the T-64 are discussed in Part 2.

The original T-64 (Object 432) in Sergievsk, Samara. This is a late production model upgraded to T-64R standard, judging by the hull. (Maksim Prikhodko, techtraveling.ru)

Ukrainian T-64A during the battles for Donetsk Airport in 2014, easily distinguishable by the coincidence rangefinder optic in front of the commander's cupola. (Andrei Tarasenko)

Firepower

Ukrainian T-64BV firing its 125mm main gun during a pre-war exercise. (ZSU)

The 2A46 (D-81) family of 125mm smoothbore guns, which include the 2A26M, 2A46, and 2A46M, was introduced on the T-64A in 1968, and variants of this family remain the main armament of all Soviet, Russian, and Ukrainian main battle tanks, so many of the characteristics discussed here remain relevant for the other tanks in this book. A list of 2A46 family projectiles likely to be encountered in the Russo–Ukrainian War is provided in Appendix 1 of Part 2.

Based on the T-62's 115mm 2A20 (U5-TS) smoothbore gun, the 2A46 family has a larger diameter in order to allow a bigger propellant charge to attain the 1,800 m/s muzzle velocity stipulated by the original 1961 requirement.[11] This was driven by the appearance of the formidable British Chieftain, whose thick frontal armour and powerful 120mm gun gave it a substantial advantage over the T-62. The T-64A started off with the 2A26M, which initially lacked a thermal sleeve and thus suffered accuracy issues due to thermal warping of the barrel. It was replaced by the 2A46-1 on later T-64A production models with a thermal sleeve.[12]

Early T-64Bs used the 2A46-2 smoothbore gun, which was modified to allow firing of the 9M112 gun-launched anti-tank guided missile (GLATGM), while from 1983 onwards T-64Bs were equipped with the 2A46M-1 introduced in 1979.[13] Despite what its name might suggest, the 2A46M had very little parts commonality with the original 2A46, and was essentially a new gun sharing only the ballistic characteristics and projectiles. It had a new barrel and redesigned breech and recoil mechanisms to allow using the 4Zh63 'super' charge with more modern ammunition such as 3BM26 *Nadezhda*-R and 3BM42 *Mango* APFSDS without adversely affecting barrel life, as well as increased accuracy due to improvements made under the *Tochnost*-2 ('Accuracy') project.[14] [15] The 2A46M variants also introduced a quick-change barrel feature, useful since serially produced Soviet, Russian, and Ukrainian 2A46M smoothbore guns do not have a chrome lining, and the barrel life is rated at just 200 APFSDS shots, comparing very poorly with Western tank guns that are usually rated for over 500.[16] The older 2A46 requires partially dismantling the turret in order to replace the barrel, a much more difficult and time-consuming operation.

The T-64 was the first Soviet tank entering service with an autoloader, officially designated the *mekhanizm zaryazhaniya* ('loading mechanism', MZ). The modernised 6ETs40-2S MZ used on the T-64B since 1979 with the 2A46M-1 gun is hydraulically powered and can hold up to 28 rounds.[17] A conveyor is located directly underneath the turret, with the rounds arranged in a circle. In order to save space, the T-64B uses two-piece rounds stored in an 'L'-shaped configuration on hinged aluminium trays, with projectiles placed horizontally on the floor of the turret, while their corresponding semi-combustible charges are stacked vertically surrounding the turret space. The gunner or commander selects the desired ammunition type (APFSDS, HE-Frag, HEAT-FS, or GLATGM) on their control panels.

The loading process takes anywhere between 6–20 seconds, depending on where the next round to be loaded is placed, since the conveyor can only rotate in one direction (clockwise).[18] If the next round is located immediately after the previous round, then the loading time is only six seconds.[19] The MZ has a 'series' mode where it will automatically load the next round in the conveyor regardless of type without the gunner's intervention. The Ukrainian tanker Aleksandr Dominikanets says it is useful in situations where a lot of shots with the same type of ammunition are needed, as it reduces operator error and thus wasted time.[20]

Although the MZ autoloader is often described as 'complex' and 'unreliable', opinions vary: SR claims that the MZ is thoroughly reliable if well-maintained, and that he has personally fired 500 rounds from T-64s and never encountered a malfunction. Dominikanets, on the other hand, considers it less reliable than

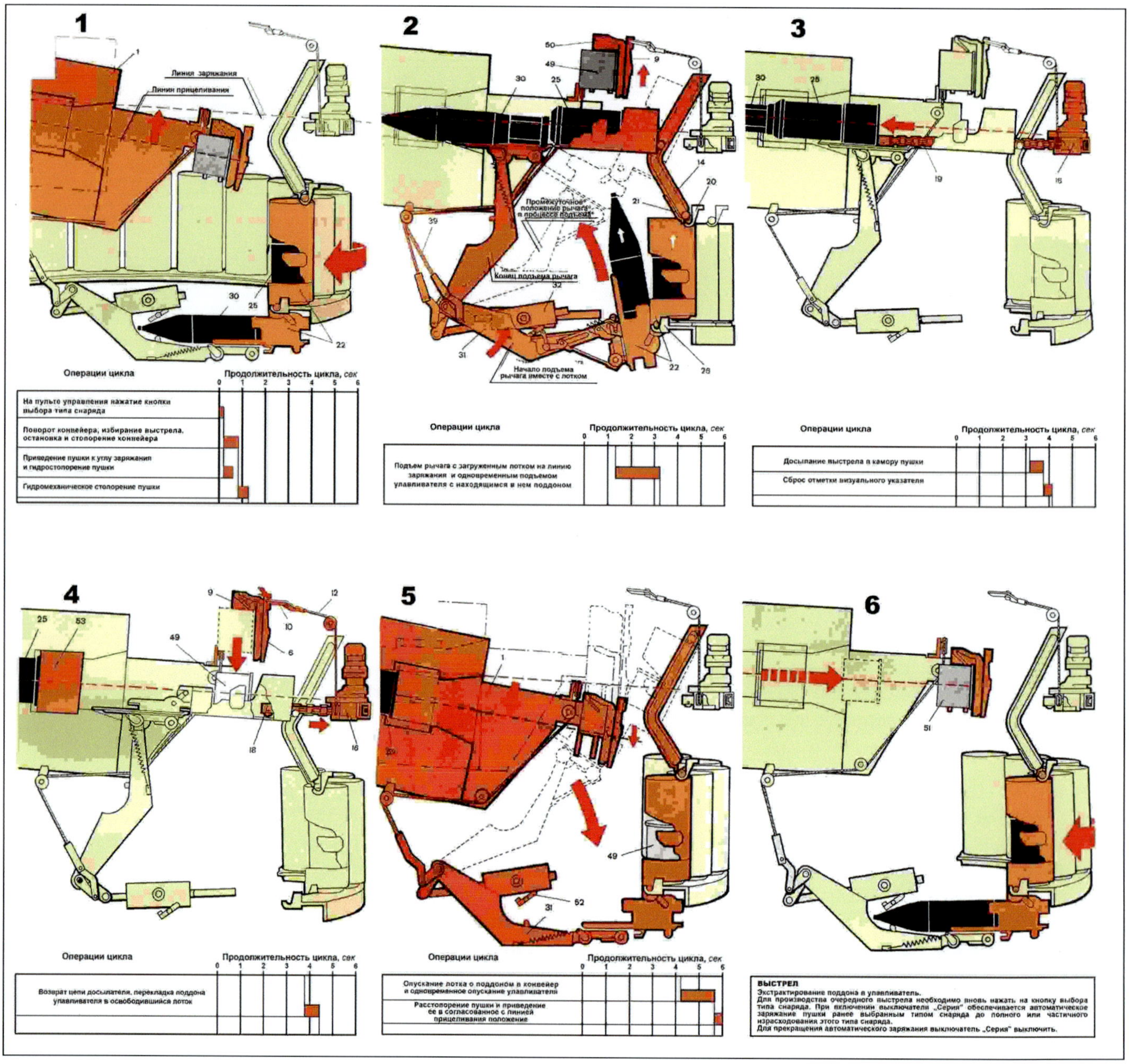

Soviet training poster illustration of the MZ's loading cycle. The entire process takes six seconds, according to the cyclogram at the bottom of each picture. (Author's collection)

the T-72's autoloader (to be described later) due to the MZ having more moving parts and a more complicated design. In the event of a malfunction, the MZ can be switched to semi-automatic mode for troubleshooting or assisted loading. Multiple reports from the Russo–Ukrainian War also indicate that the autoloader can jam if the tank is hit, even if it is not penetrated. If the MZ is disabled, has no ammunition, or is otherwise non-functional for any reason, the gun can be manually loaded by the commander, although it will obviously take significantly longer.

The MZ also has an illuminated ammo counter located on the commander's station. Dominikanets considers it to be quite handy, and makes it easy to spot what he calls *zaytsev* ('hares'; Russian slang for stowaway): errors in the autoloader's memory unit where it records the presence of a round in a tray that is actually empty. This can cause obvious problems in combat, but can also damage the autoloader.

Restocking the carousel is relatively straightforward, essentially the loading process in reverse. Restocking all 28 rounds takes 13–15 minutes according to the manual: Saenko says based on personal experience that it can be done much faster (around 7 minutes) with some minor shortcuts.[21] Dominikanets also notes that it is physically easier for the commander to manually stow and retrieve rounds in a T-64B than in a T-72B. The T-64B carries a total of 36 rounds: of the remaining eight rounds, seven are stored to the right of the driver, and one in the turret.[22]

The T-64B's FCS is the 1A33-1 *Ob*. It includes the 1G42 gunner primary sight with integral 9S517 laser rangefinder, 1V517 analogue ballistic computer, 1G43 shot release block, 2E42 gun stabiliser, 1B11 crosswind sensor, and 1B14 roll sensor. The *Ob* FCS has fully automatic lead and elevation compensation: all the gunner has to do once the target has been 'lased' is keep the aiming chevron in the 1G42 sight on the target; the FCS will automatically adjust the gun and turret to compensate. His sight picture is not displaced thanks to the sight's independent two-plane stabilisation.[23] The *Ob*'s maximum range in direct-fire mode is 4km, though the T-64B can conduct indirect fire with HE-Frag projectiles out to about 10km using firing tables and manual gunnery.

1A33 *Ob* FCS components (excluding gun stabiliser). The 1G42 gunner sight is in the middle background. (TsKB Tochpribor)

T-64Bs fitted with the 9K112-1 *Kobra* guided missile complex can use the 9M112 family of GLATGMs. These are radio-command guided missiles, relying on command signals generated by the 9S416-1 system linked with the *Ob* FCS and 1G42 sight and transmitted by the GTN-12 antenna transmitter. The 9M112 family uses semi-automatic command to line-of-sight (SACLOS) guidance, thus the gunner must keep the aiming chevron of the 1G42 sight on-target until the missile hits. They can also be used to engage helicopters in addition to armoured vehicles. T-64Bs that are 'fitted for but not with' the *Kobra* complex are designated 'T-64B1' (Object 437A). These do not have the GTN-12 antenna block in front of the commander's cupola.

These advanced gunnery features did not come cheap: a T-64B with the full weapons suite cost 70 percent more than a T-64A, while a T-64B1 with only the *Ob* FCS cost 40 percent more.[24] However, Soviet studies showed that a fully automatic FCS like the *Ob* reduced target engagement times by 30–40 percent compared to a partially automated FCS like that used on the T-64A and Cold War T-72 models, and by over 50 percent compared to the primitive manual FCS of the T-62.[25] The Soviets thus judged it to be a worthwhile improvement.

In addition to the 1G42 sight, the gunner has access to the TPN-1-49-23 night/auxiliary monocular periscopic sight. This is an image intensifier sight relying on active illumination from the L-4A *Luna-2* infrared (IR) searchlight, although it can also operate in passive mode, which cuts the vision range in half. On T-64s, the searchlight is mounted to the left of the main gun, unlike the T-72 and T-80.[26] The T-64's night sight is mechanically linked to the 1G42 and thus shares the same stabilisation. By 1978, Western tanks were starting to appear with greatly superior thermal imaging sights, but it would be almost 40 years before the T-64B would get a thermal sight in the 2017 Ukrainian modernisation programme, described separately.

The 125mm main gun is complemented by a 7.62mm PKT coaxial machine gun located to its right. The T-64B also has a 12.7mm NSVT *Utyos* ('Cliff') heavy anti-aircraft machine gun (AAMG) on a ZU-64A mounting controlled by the commander. The ZU-64A is

ZU-64A AAMG mounting and cupola. On the right, the commander of a T-64BM2 (which uses the same cupola) fires his *Utyos* AAMG without exposing himself. (NMFTE Telegram)

remotely controlled and the commander can aim and fire it using the PZU-5 monocular periscopic sight without exposing himself. However, he must still expose himself in order to reload it.

The commander's primary sight is the TKN-3VM combined day/night pseudo-binocular periscopic sight. It can operate in both passive and active night modes: in active mode it works with the OU-3GKU IR searchlight mounted to the left of the *Utyos* AAMG. The cupola is horizontally stabilised with the 1ETs40-2S electromechanical drive via a counter-rotating mechanism when set to 'hold' mode. However, the commander has to elevate or depress the TKN-3VM manually with a handle. The commander can also use the TKN-3VM to designate targets for the gunner by overriding the turret traverse, although he has no means to control the gun's elevation and thus cannot conduct gunnery by himself. In general, the T-64 commander's vision while 'buttoned down' is quite limited compared to Western tanks or in the T-72, since there are only three other periscopes to look outside and their fields-of-view are restricted.

Protection

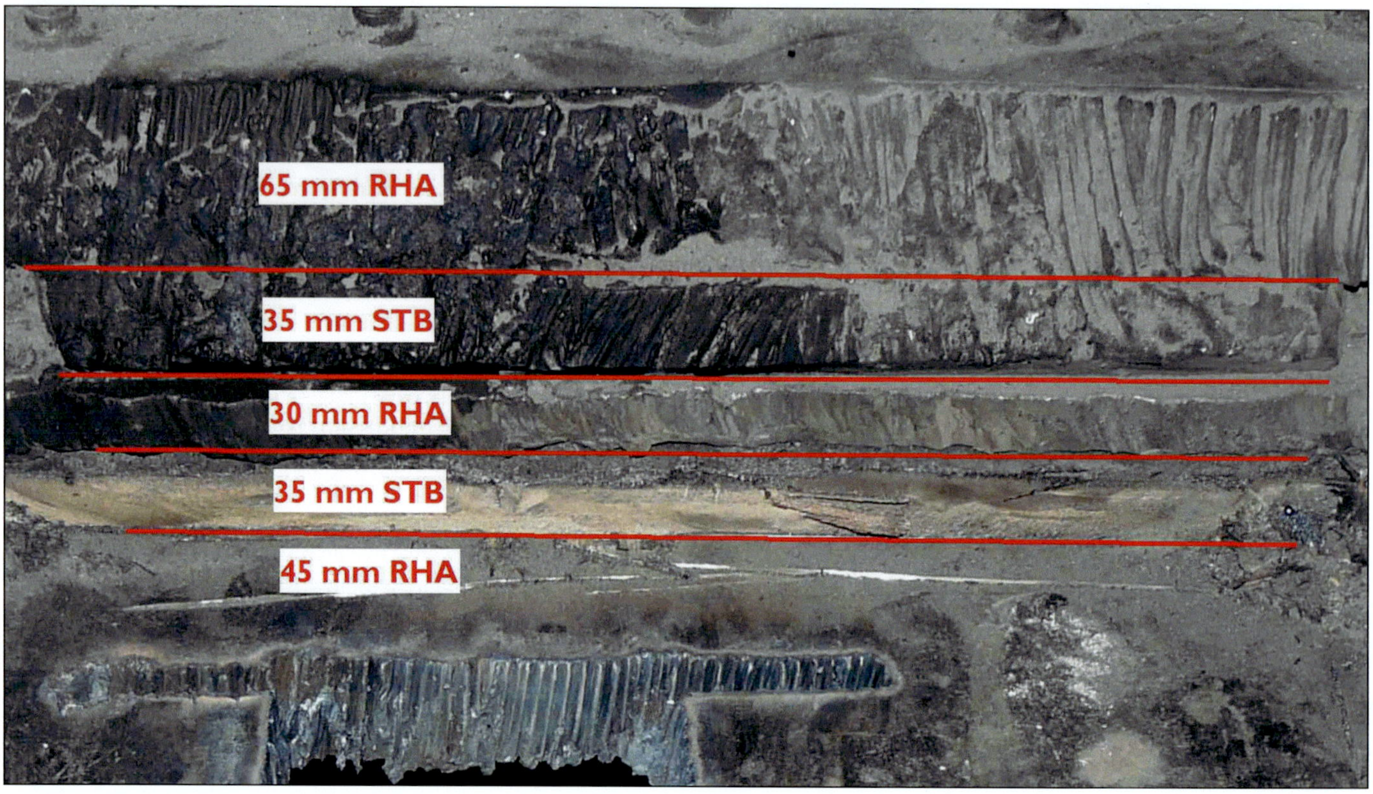

Cutaway of a post-1984 T-64B's upper glacis composite armour. (Andrei Tarasenko)

The T-64 was the world's first serial production tank with composite armour.[27] On the T-64A and early T-64Bs, the frontal hull upper glacis protection consisted of a sandwich with 80mm RHA facing outwards, 20mm of RHA as the internal backing plate, and two 52.5mm layers of STB armour-grade fibreglass in between, mounted at 68° from the vertical. This arrangement is often known as the '80-105-20' composite armour, and it was also used on early T-72 and T-80 tanks. When it first appeared in 1964, the Soviets rated it sufficiently protective against contemporary armour-piercing discarding sabot (APDS) ammunition from the ubiquitous NATO 105mm tank gun.

However, during the 1982 Lebanon War, the Syrian Arab Army captured some brand new Israeli M111 *Hetz* 105mm APFSDS. M111 *Hetz* used a monobloc tungsten alloy penetrator and had much improved penetration against sloped armour compared to previous APFSDS rounds. It easily perforated contemporary Soviet tanks, including those with the '80-105-20' glacis. This led to an armour improvement research programme codenamed *Otrazhenie* ('Reflection'), which sought both an interim solution for current tanks and a long-term solution for future production tanks. The former was adopted in 1983 through a 30mm RHA applique plate added to the upper glacis of existing T-64s.

The long-term solution came in 1984 with a new five-layer upper glacis composite sandwich consisting of 65mm RHA, 35mm STB, 30mm high hardness armour (HHA), 35mm STB, and 45mm RHA backing plate.[28] This configuration significantly increased the upper glacis' protection against APFSDS and other kinetic projectiles. At the same time, the new glacis configuration's resistance against shaped charge warheads was rated as somewhat lower than the original '80-105-20' glacis, but this was more than compensated for by the addition of *Kontakt*-1 explosive reactive armour (ERA) on the T-64BV and T-64B1V in 1985. There is, however, a weakened zone around the driver's hatch where there is no composite armour due to the unavoidable need to make space for the driver's position. This weakness is present on the T-72 and T-80 families as well.[29]

The T-64B's turret is also protected by composite armour in the frontal aspect, though it is of a different composition to the upper glacis. It is made of cast steel with cavities containing 70mm-diameter KVP-98 spheres made of a ceramic material known as '*ultrafarfor*' (lit. 'ultra-porcelain') derived from a mixture of alumina, clay, and barium oxide, suspended in MBL-1 cast steel.[30] The manufacturing process results in an ultra-hard mullite-corundum composite, and thus the *ultrafarfor* spheres are also sometimes referred to as 'corundum spheres'.[31] The line-of-sight (LOS) thickness varies due to the rounded shape of the turret,[32] but according to Tarasenko it is 400–475mm frontally (nominally 115mm steel, 140mm ultrafarfor/MBL-1, and 135mm steel).[33] The original T-64 entered service with a cast steel turret with a very thick aluminium filler (turret LOS thickness ~600mm), required to achieve the desired protection level. It meant that the turret would block the driver's hatch when traversed at certain angles.[34] This and other problems led to the T-64A being introduced with a new turret using high-hardness steel inserts in 1968.[35] Once its manufacturing process was mastered, the ceramic-sphere turret was introduced on T-64As produced from 1974 onwards and unified with the T-64B.[36]

During trials in 1967, ceramic-sphere turrets successfully withstood HEAT-FS from the 100mm 2A19 smoothbore anti-tank gun, APDS from the 100mm D-10 rifled gun, and APFSDS from the 115mm 2A20 smoothbore gun without any penetrations. This was judged sufficient against the best 105mm projectiles of the time. Protection against shaped charge projectiles was further enhanced by the addition of *Kontakt*-1 ERA on the T-64BV. Despite this, the ceramic-sphere turret was not adopted for the T-72 and T-80 tanks because the other Soviet tank factories were unable/unwilling to master the production method, as well as lingering quality control problems and the development of better armour layouts.

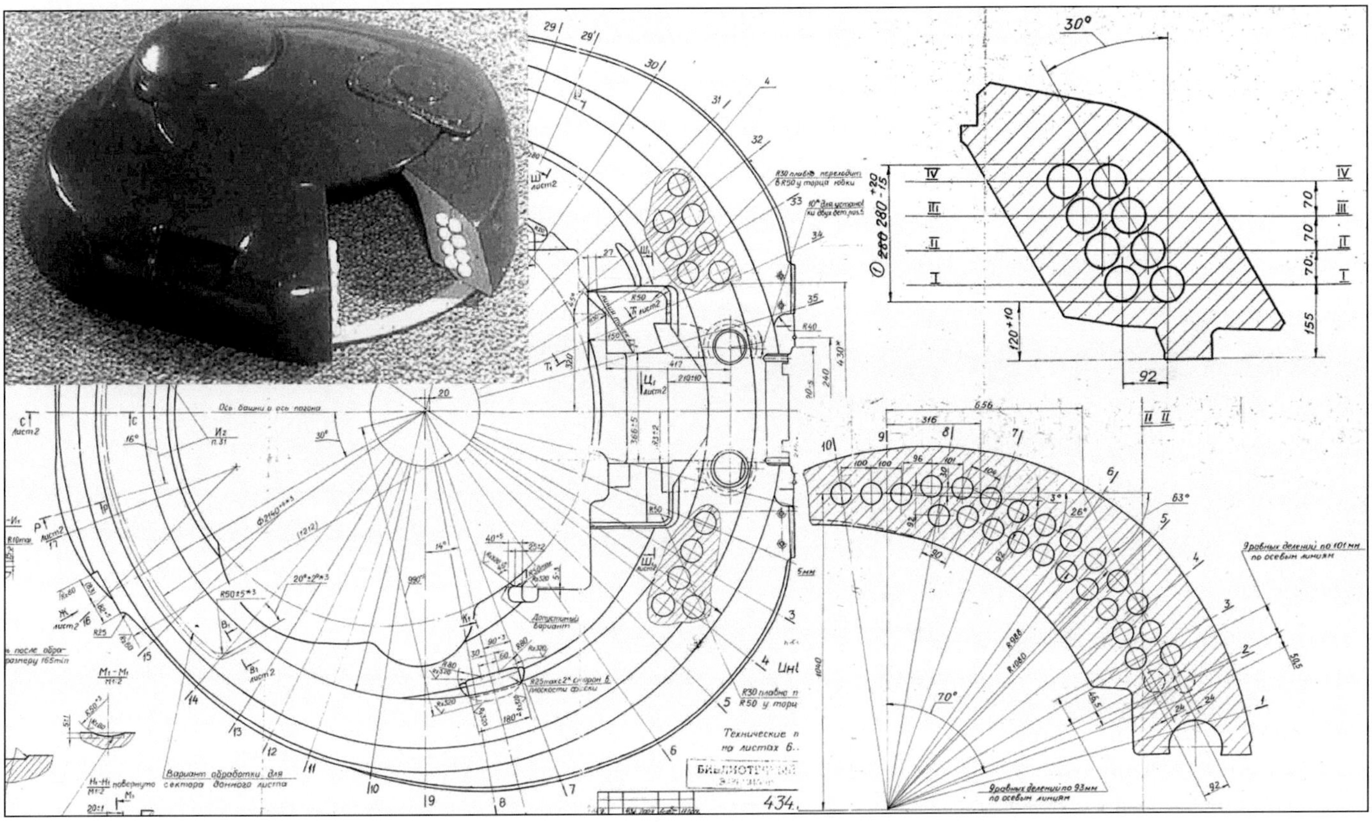

Cross-sections from 1978 T-64A turret blueprints showing the placement of the ceramic spheres. Inset: model of the T-64B turret. (Andrei Tarasenko)

The T-64BV *Kontakt*-1 ERA package consists of 265 blocks: 80 on the frontal turret, 99 on the frontal hull, and the remainder on the forward half of each side of the tank. It covers about 70 percent and 62 percent of the frontal area projections of the T-64B's hull and turret, respectively, and weighs about two tonnes. Unlike other Soviet tanks, the *Kontakt*-1 protecting the side of the T-64BV hull was not attached directly to the flimsy side-skirts; rather, it was mounted on much sturdier frames fixed to the hull. While heavier, this arrangement was much less prone to losing ERA bricks during movement than the side-skirt-mounted *Kontakt*-1 arrangement.[37] In 1982 tests, a T-64B equipped with *Kontakt*-1 was tested against the 125mm 3BK14M HEAT-FS shell, 9M114 *Kokon* anti-tank guided missile (ATGM), and 9M112 GLATGM. The combined ERA and composite armour prevented any penetrations into the crew compartment along the frontal aspect, requiring only the replacement of knocked off/expended ERA blocks and relatively minor repairs to the tank.[38]

One feature introduced on the T-64 and kept by all subsequent Soviet tanks is the built-in retractable dozer blade mounted on the lower hull. This allows it to dig its own 'hull-down' position for defensive purposes. The T-64B is also equipped with the 902B *Tucha*-1 system with eight 3D6 smoke grenade launchers. On early T-64Bs, they are mounted on the turret face, four on each side of the main gun. With the addition of ERA, they were relocated to the left side of the turret, next to the gunner's hatch. The T-64 also has the ability to create its own smokescreen by injecting fuel into the engine exhaust manifold.[39]

T-64B during exercises in 2020. This is an unusual specimen with the side hull frames for mounting *Kontakt*-1 ERA but appears to be an older 1970s-production T-64B with stowage boxes on the turret front. (Pivnich.org.ua)

Mobility

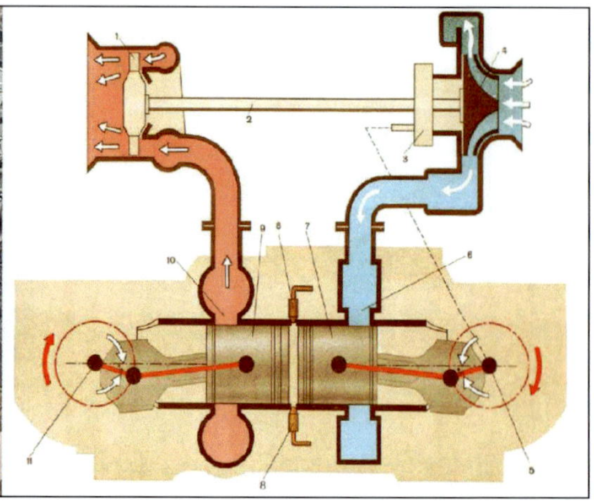

The 'heart' of the T-64: the 700hp 5TDF opposed-piston engine. The cross-section from a Soviet technical poster shows the main cylinder and the turbo-supercharger. (SR and author's collection)

The T-64 uses the 5TDF two-stroke five-cylinder turbo-supercharged liquid-cooled multi-fuel diesel engine, rated at 700hp.[40] Developed by the aero-engine designer Andrey Charomsky and inspired by the German Junkers Jumo 205 aircraft diesel engine of the 1930s, the 5TDF is an opposed-piston engine.[41] This effectively allows one to fit 10 pistons into an engine of comparable size to a five-cylinder engine, resulting in a very compact engine. The 5TDF is a multi-fuel engine, and can operate on high-speed diesel fuel, kerosene jet fuel, gasoline, or any mixture of these fuels. However, it is quite finicky in terms of acceptable fuel quality, and some types are preferred in certain temperature regimes.

The two-stroke cycle helped squeeze as much power as possible. Each 5TDF cylinder is configured in such a way that the ports for the compressed air and the exhaust are on opposite sides of the cylinder. This allows it to use 'uniflow scavenging': fresh air and exhaust gases move in a single direction through the cylinder during the scavenging process, minimising any mixing of the exhaust and fresh air/fuel mixture, further improving engine efficiency. A hybrid turbo-supercharger is used to provide compressed air for the combustion chamber, with the supercharger driven by the engine itself and the exhaust used to drive a turbine connected to the supercharger fan for increased efficiency. As with most Soviet tanks, the engine can be started electrically using a starter-generator or with compressed air.

Unlike the previous Soviet medium tanks, there is no radiator cooling fan: the T-64 uses an 'ejection cooling mechanism' where the ejection of exhaust from the engine itself is used to create suction within the engine compartment to draw in cooling air for the liquid coolant radiator.[42] This saves space and weight and has no moving parts. The opposed-piston configuration also results in lower specific heat transfer through the cylinder walls into the oil and coolant, which in turn means the 5TDF is a lot more tolerant of hot ambient temperatures without power loss than the T-72's V-12 diesel engines.[43]

The 5TDF also uses a novel two-stage cassetteless air cleaning system. The first stage relies on inertial separation on an inertial grating. The second stage uses cyclonic action, akin to how a Dyson bagless vacuum cleaner works, with the dust being blown out using engine exhaust. There are a few reasons for this system: first, it saves space; second, it removes the need to clean at set periods (in theory: the manual still says it has to be cleaned 'as needed'); third, two-stroke engines with uniflow scavenging like the 5TDF are sensitive to intake airflow disruption, and a filter would have reduced the engine's efficiency significantly; finally, it helps protect the tank from attack by incendiary weapons such as Molotov cocktails or napalm, which was a requirement imposed on KhKBM by the Soviet military.[44] Flexible dust deflectors are also installed beside the air intake.

Conversely, these systems impose a greater relative power cost on the engine due to the greater intake resistance than previous systems. A 1985 study notes that the T-64 has a higher relative power cost (12.8 percent) than the more conservatively designed T-72 (11.5 percent), although at ambient temperatures above 30°C the T-72's cooling system becomes less efficient and the power cost is higher (14.3 percent). Despite this, the T-64's power plant still had the highest power density among contemporary tanks (T-72, M60, Leopards 1 and 2) by a considerable margin.[45]

With all the new technologies and innovations implemented, the 5TDF's reliability in service was (unsurprisingly) initially poor, with the 1967 factory warranty set at an abysmal 150 hours. Perfecting the 5TDF was a protracted affair.[46] By 1976, with experience and continued development, the warranty and pre-overhaul engine life of the 5TDF reached 500 hours, fully satisfying Soviet requirements. Unfortunately for Morozov, his rivals had used these early problems as a platform to lobby for their own alternative designs, the T-72 and T-80, a story for later. It has also led to the T-64's enduring reputation for being an unreliable tank, especially when compared to the T-72.

To quote Sergey Suvorov, an ex-T-64 tank company commander, the 5TDF is 'not designed for fools': it requires correct by-the-book maintenance in order to work reliably. In an army primarily made up of conscripts with relatively low training and/or mechanical knowledge, to say that this was challenging would be an understatement.[47] According to Suvorov, the two most common failure modes for the 5TDF are overheating and dust damage, both usually caused by a failure to follow the manual.[48] In a two-stroke engine, combustion occurs with every revolution of the crankshaft, instead of with every other revolution for four-stroke engines. This means more heat generated and the engine is therefore very dependent on its liquid cooling system working properly. Like any engine, the 5TDF's cooling system requires distilled water, but it was not uncommon for driver-mechanics to simply ignore this and use tap water instead. This would result in mineral scale build-up in the thin channels of the cooling system, causing overheating and engine failure.

Dust damage was usually caused by dust-trapping lubricant oil build-up in the air cleaner: some crews misinterpreted 'clean as needed' in the manual as 'no need for cleaning'. The oil itself usually came from spillage, since the lubricant port was located next to the air intake, or from ingesting exhaust or vapours from other tanks. According to Suvorov, one just has to check the inlets and dust ejection pipe for oil, and clean if necessary. He was also able to negate the oil spillage problem completely by using a rubber mat to cover the intake during refilling. The driver also has to be somewhat careful in handling the engine, since frequent sudden changes in engine RPM can cause turbulence in the cyclonic action, resulting in dust being sucked into the engine.

Irrespective of the problems associated with early manufacturing defects and poor crew training, the 5TDF also has drawbacks inherent in its design. Because its oil-coated pistons also act as inlet/exhaust valves, the 5TDF loses lubricant oil during combustion, which means it generally requires more oil than a four-stroke engine. For comparison, based on a 1976 trial involving 300km daily marches, a T-64A consumed about 10 percent more fuel than a T-72 but almost 100 percent more lubricant oil on average.[49] The 5TDF (₽18,000) also cost almost double the T-72B's V-84 engine (₽9,800) and was more complex to mass-produce.[50]

Diesel engines like the 5TDF also do not have spark plugs and rely only on the compression of the fuel-air mixture by the piston to ignite it; the colder the engine, the more difficult it is to ignite the mixture. The 5TDF is even more difficult to start in cold weather than the V-12 diesels without assistance because of its two-stroke cycle, high operating temperature, and use of uniflow scavenging with (cold) air fed from the supercharger. As one might imagine, this is suboptimal for a Soviet tank, but it was remedied in 1978 with the introduction of direct oil injection and an 'autonomous flame heating system', a mini flamethrower that heats the intake air. It allows the T-64 to be reliably started from as cold as -25°C, at the cost of increased fuel and oil consumption.

The 5TDF's power output remained unchanged even as successive models of the T-64 gained more weight, and the power/weight ratio dropped from a respectable 19.4 horsepower per tonne (hp/t) for the original T-64 (36 tonnes) to about 16.5hp/t for the T-64BV (41 tonnes), the lowest of the first-line Soviet main battle tanks of the 1980s.[51] This naturally had an adverse effect on the tank's mobility, especially acceleration. The improved 1,000hp six-cylinder 6TD-1 opposed-piston engine was intended to replace the 5TD. It was successfully tested in the prototype Object 476 tanks under the *Kedr* ('Cedar') programme, which also implemented numerous other improvements to the T-64. The 6TD-1 was adopted for service in 1983 and it was intended that the entire T-64A/B fleet would be upgraded with the new engine, but this was never carried out because the gas turbine-powered T-80 was favoured by Minister of Defence Dmitriy Ustinov.[52] It would be almost four decades before a T-64 with the 6TD-1 would enter actual service in the form of the T-64BM2, to be discussed later.

The T-64's hydraulic-mechanical transmission is also radically different from that of preceding Soviet tanks. Instead of having separate planetary and input gearboxes, clutch, brakes, and final drives, the T-64 combines all the transmission elements into a compact seven-speed unit known as a 'BKP' (*bortovie korobki peredach* — 'side gearbox') located on each side of the 5TDF engine. The BKP consists of only two nodes: the planetary gearbox and the final drive. Since it is directly attached to the engine, there is no need for a separate input gearbox like on older Soviet tanks. The result is that the T-64's transmission is 750kg lighter than the nine-unit transmission of the T-55, and also contains only 150 machined parts compared to 500 on the T-55.[53] Similar BKP units would also be adopted for all future Soviet, Russian, and Ukrainian tanks.

Steering is accomplished by simply switching the BKP on one side to a different gear from the BKP on the other side. This is done using the steering lever connected to the BKP by a hydraulic servo-mechanism. Because the final drives are directly attached to the drive wheels and engine via the BKP, there is relatively little power loss compared to older transmissions. The seven forward gears and one reverse gear give a maximum forward road speed of 60.5km/h but a maximum reverse speed of only 4.8km/h. At the time, Soviet tank doctrine and tactics did not place great value in having a high reverse speed, but this has been recognised as a significant drawback in more recent times, particularly based on combat experience.[54]

The BKPs are not without their drawbacks. Unlike previous Soviet tank transmissions, the BKPs gave different turn radii at different

A left-side T-64 BKP (432.48.020sb-2). Bottom shows how the BKPs are attached to the 5TDF engine and drive wheels. (SR and author's collection)

gear settings. It is generally better for a tank to have progressively larger turning radii with increasing gear settings (i.e. higher speeds) for smoother turns. However, the turning radii for the T-64 change erratically with increasing gears and actually *decrease* from Gear IV onwards. For Gears VI and VII, the turning radii are impossibly small, which results in jerky turns and skidding at high speeds. This drawback also means that in order to achieve a larger turning radius at higher speeds, the driver has to adjust the steering lever several times to make multiple smaller turns. This increases driver workload and also results in a greater speed loss during turns. Comparative tests conducted at Kubinka between a T-64A and a tank with two-line differential gear and steering (M48A3) showed that the T-64A lost more speed during turns.[55]

The 5TDF and BKPs are very compact, allowing the T-64 to have the smallest engine compartment of any existing tank. It also means they are relatively easy to remove for maintenance or replacement compared to previous Soviet tanks. The T-64's engine compartment is divided into two 'decks', with the engine and transmission in the lower deck. The upper deck contains the ejection cooling system, the exhaust system, the transmission lubricant supply system, and air intakes; these are integrated into the engine compartment roof. According to the repair manual, complete engine

The T-64's engine compartment. The 1.5 tonne roof must be secured with a special latch: failure to do so has had fatal consequences on more than one occasion, according to Chobitok. (SR)

replacement requires 38 man-hours; with relatively easy access to most components (for a Soviet tank) it can be done in 13 hours by three men.[56]

Morozov also adopted a completely new lightweight torsion bar suspension system and chassis for the T-64. Externally, its most distinctive feature is the small-diameter road wheels with internal rubber shock absorbers. The rims are made of steel, with the hub assembly from aluminium alloy.[57] The use of internal rubber shock absorbers subjected them to less environmental wear compared to conventional rubber tyres and made the wheels more resistant to damage from napalm or nuclear blast/heat effects. These wheels are unique to the T-64 family (which includes the BM *Bulat* and T-64BM2).[58] They are also relatively thin, which helps them 'cut' through muddy soil like a knife through butter and maintain contact with the tracks.

The road wheels are mounted on long torsion keys (balancers) that connect them to the torsion bars. The first road wheel is mounted slightly higher than the others, reducing the load on it and causing it to sink less deeply when entering mud.[59] The return rollers per side and front idler wheel also have internal shock absorbers: the latter is interchangeable with the road wheels. The rear drive sprocket, directly connected to the BKP transmission unit, and has a characteristic mud scraper located just in front of and between the rims.

Close-up of the T-64's suspension. The small-diameter road wheels, long torsion keys, telescopic shock absorbers, and unique track design are readily apparent. The front idler wheels are interchangeable with the road wheels. (Bogdan Mayboroda)

The most unique feature of the T-64's suspension is, in fact, its torsion bars. Most Cold War and some modern MBTs use torsion bar suspensions because they are relatively weight- and space-efficient and simple. These work by using the twisting of a metal rod (the torsion bar) to absorb the vertical motion of the attached road wheel, the torsion key acting as a lever. The allowed twist angle is proportional to the bar's length and rigidity. In the vast majority of tanks, these bars span the full width of the hull, with the attachment points for a wheel's torsion bar on the opposite side of the hull. The wheels on opposite sides have to be offset in order to fit. However, the T-64 uses half-length coaxial torsion bars attached to the middle of the hull, with no offset between wheels of opposing sides. A special pre-setting process is used to twist and then heat-treat the bars, resulting in plastic deformations on the hardened surface and elastic deformations in the core. The result is that the core is in a state of tension with the hardened surface, trying to untwist itself. These pre-stressed bars are then installed in such a way that the upward movement of the road wheel twists the bar in the *opposite* direction to its internal twist.[60] This allows for greater shear stresses and therefore a larger twist angle than otherwise possible for a torsion bar of its length.[61] It also means that torsion bars for opposing sides of the tank are not interchangeable.

The T-64 also uses its own unique dual-pin tracks, distinct from the single-pin tracks of the T-62 and T-72 or the dual-pin tracks of later Soviet tanks. Each track section has two stamped steel pads, each with a hole in the middle. This prevents mud from accumulating as quickly on the tracks by allowing it to squeeze/fall out through the holes. They improve traction in mud: consider snowshoes, which have holes that improve traction but mean lower bearing capacity in snow compared to skis. Skis, however, tend to skid in snow: desirable for skiers, not so much for a tank. The T-64's tracks are a compromise between snowshoes and skis, whereas the T-72 and T-80 have tracks that act more like skis.[62]

As a result, the T-64's tracks have significantly better grip on muddy terrain and are also significantly lighter than conventional tracks, thus less power is wasted moving the track itself. However, these tracks require more effort to repair and replace than single-pin tracks due to the more complex design (six man-hours for T-64 vs. four for T-72 for replacement). The section pieces are joined together by a concave-shaped shoe in the middle with a guide and two binocular-shaped brackets on the ends, fastened together by two parallel track pins.

The track pin of the T-64 is known in Russian as a 'rubber-metal joint' (*rezino-metallicheskiy sharnir*, RMSh). It derives its name from the rubber bushings around the metal rod of the track pin, which causes the 'live' tracks to bend inwards by themselves. Strictly speaking, RMSh is not a formal designation for the tracks. Dual-pin 'live' tracks like the T-64's are known as 'parallel RMSh' (*parallelniy RMSh*) tracks, while single-pin 'live' tracks like those used on the T-62 and T-72 are called 'sequential RMSh' (*posledovatelniy RMSh*) tracks.[63]

The end result of these design decisions is that the T-64 has considerably better cross-country mobility in European terrain, especially soft soils like clay, mud, peat, or chernozem, than the T-72 or T-80. This was demonstrated repeatedly in trials and in service. In a spring 1974 test, the T-64 was able to make multiple passages through a swamp with a depth of 0.85–1.2m with no troubles, while the T-72 and the T-80 both got stuck at least once. The T-64 could even cross a swamp with a depth of 1.2–1.5m without getting stuck, which proved beyond the T-72 and T-80.[64] It is worth noting that the T-64 has a height of only 2.1m, and its ground clearance is only ~0.5m. Another example is a 1976 test where all three types were tested crossing a 'swamp' (mud depth greater than vehicle ground clearance). Out of 11 crossings, the T-64 did not get stuck a single time, while the T-80 and T-72 got stuck in three of 13 and four of 12 attempts, respectively.[65]

As always, there are trade-offs: The thin road wheels can also become a liability if the tracks come off for any reason (combat damage, mishandling, etc.) while driving through mud or loose dirt/sand. Since the wheels have greater ground pressure, the tank will sink in more deeply. A 1974 test of such a scenario showed that a T-64 required nearly 20 tonne-force (tf) to pull out in loose dirt, nearly four times the T-72 (4.9tf) and over twice the T-80 (8.2tf). This would require a dedicated armoured recovery vehicle to recover the tank.[66] The T-64's tracks and road wheels are also significantly inferior to the T-72's in terms of traction in sand, and the suspension can also experience vibration problems when running on hard asphalt roads or concrete.[67]

The first, second, and sixth suspension units are fitted with double-acting telescopic hydraulic shock absorbers. These are significantly more efficient than the hydraulic vane shock absorbers used on previous Soviet tanks (and T-72) and have a much larger force limit (90kN vs 40kN).[68] The trade-off is that the T-64's shock absorbers generate more heat: early versions suffered from overheating of the hydraulic fluid, but this was fixed with a thermal valve. The combination of small wheels with internal shock absorbers, efficient hydraulic shock absorbers, special torsion bars, and long torsion keys (~50 percent longer than the T-72's) results in a softer suspension, giving the T-64 the smoothest ride out of all the Soviet MBTs on moderately bumpy soft soil and dirt roads. This significantly improves crew comfort and gunnery while moving on such terrain.[69]

It is often said that the T-64's chassis is complex, unreliable, and expensive. In fact, Klimov et al.'s report concludes, based on test results gathered between 1976–1984, that the T-64's chassis is more reliable and much cheaper than the T-72 or T-80's. It is also the lightest and has the lowest power loss among the three types.[70] A comparison between the T-64 and T-72 based on their manuals also shows that it is significantly easier to replace and maintain most of the T-64's chassis components compared to the T-72.[71]

Context

Given how radically different the T-64 is to earlier tanks like the T-62, it is quite easy to forget that the original T-62 and T-64 models entered service within only a few years of each other. T-64BV production ended in 1987, which means that even the 'youngest' T-64BV still in service is at least 35 years old as of 2022. Against today's Western MBTs and even modernised Russian MBTs such as the T-72B3, T-90A/M, and T-80BVM, an unmodernised T-64BV cannot honestly be said to be a match in a head-to-head fight. Most acutely, the base armour protection is no longer sufficient to reasonably protect against modern anti-tank weapons.

It also lacks features that would be considered essential in a modern Western tank, such as thermal imaging sights for the gunner and the commander. While innovative and efficient for its day, the mobility never received any significant upgrades over the years and the T-64BV is underpowered and relatively taxing to drive in an era where the latest tanks have 1,500+ hp engines and automatic transmissions. The poor reverse speed is also a significant hindrance, forcing the tank to either turn around and expose its weaker side and rear armour or reverse at a painfully slow pace, a serious disadvantage when needing to back off from an engagement.

Nevertheless, the T-64BV, even without modernisation, does have things it can bring to the table. Its 125mm gun, while no

This 'separatist' T-64BV bears the marking 'N-0200', a Russian railway system marker code, indicating that it was sent to the 'separatists' from Russia. Russia continues to deny its involvement in this phase of the war to this day. (Vitaly Kuzmin)

longer top-of-the-line as a tank killer, is still a highly lethal weapon. Tanks have a lot more roles beyond simply dueling against other tanks, such as supporting infantry against enemy strongpoints and fortifications, for which the HE-Frag shell is more important. The standard 125mm 3OF26 HE-Frag shell contains 3.4kg of A-IX-2 high explosive.[72] To put this into perspective, the standard 53-OF-462 HE-Frag shell for 122mm D-30 (2A18) howitzers has 3.67kg of TNT, a weaker explosive.[73] HE-Frag shells can also be effective against other MBTs. The explosion upon impact can concuss the crew, induce them to abandon the vehicle, damage vital systems such as optics and electronics, or set fire to external fuel tanks, rendering the tank unable to fight. More serious structural damage is also possible if it hits the right area.

The T-64 may also be the tank best suited for the fighting in Ukraine in terms of its cross-country capabilities. As noted before, Morozov and his team optimised the T-64's suspension and tracks for European operations, especially in mud. During the spring and fall rainy seasons, the Ukrainian *chernozem* (lit. 'black soil') becomes a nigh-impassable morass as it gets waterlogged. This is the notorious *rasputitsa* or, to use the Ukrainian term, *bezdorizhzhia* ('roadlessness') season, which has proven to be the bane of attacking armies since the time of the Kievan Rus in the thirteenth century. The T-64 is likely to better cope with such conditions: it does not mean that T-64s are completely immune to mud, but that the Ukrainian T-64s would have more freedom of movement than the Russian T-72/T-80/T-90 tanks, especially during the muddy seasons.

Many of the T-64s that the Soviet Union had were based in Ukraine for logistical reasons, since the tank was designed and built in Kharkov (today Kharkiv). Thus, when Ukraine gained its independence in 1991, it inherited 2,340 T-64 tanks, of which 1,574 were T-64Bs.[74] It was decided that the T-72s and T-80s would be put into storage. According to ex-HUR employee Colonel Dmitriy Sobolev, in 2014, Ukraine had approximately 700 tanks in active service.[75] The vast majority of these were unmodernised T-64Bs (~600), subtracting the 85 *Bulats*. At the start of the Donbas War, the ZSU's T-64 fleet was in a decrepit state. The poor Ukrainian economy meant that there was no funding to refurbish the tanks throughout the 20 years before 2014. Components such as electronics and rubber sealants used in the engine and transmission failed as they had been left in a state of disrepair or degraded due to their age. Ammunition and the explosives in the *Kontakt*-1 ERA blocks were often found to be age-expired; the former caused accuracy problems and the latter led to some unnecessary losses. The on-board automatic fire extinguisher for the engine also often did not work, which led to more preventable losses.[76] However, when the ERA did actually work, the T-64BV proved fairly resilient against most of the old Soviet weapons used by the 'separatist' forces. According to Serhiy Zgurets, director of the Ukrainian defence publication *Defense Express*, 57 of roughly 70 ZSU tanks irrecoverably destroyed in 2014 were identified to be T-64BVs.[77]

The so-called Luhansk and Donetsk People's Republics (LNR and DNR, respectively) also use T-64s. Some were captured from the ZSU, but in June 2014, after numerous defeats, Russia began providing tanks to them. Initially, T-64s were sent in order to preserve a degree of plausible deniability, since the VSRF had retired it from service in the 2000s and the separatists could claim that they had captured these tanks from military warehouses. Jaroslaw Wolski estimates the separatists received 70–80 T-64s from Russia between June–November 2014 and lost 41 of them between 2014–2017. After November, Russia exclusively sent T-72s instead, as the pool of serviceable T-64s in Russian storage was mostly exhausted.[78]

Despite the T-64's age, before the 2022 invasion the ZSU had stated that it planned to keep the T-64 in service until 2045.[79] It had implemented a modest modernisation program, which to be described later, and was in the process of developing a comprehensive modernisation programme known as '*Krab*' for the T-64 that was to have been unveiled in 2022. It is currently unknown if the ZSU still intends to keep the T-64 in service once the war is over. After the Donbas War broke out, Ukraine began returning its stored T-72 and T-80 tanks into service, but the T-64 family still formed the bulk of the ZSU tank force in February 2022. The Association of Ukrainian Defense Manufacturers (AUDM) estimates Ukraine had 800–900 tanks in February 2021.[80] In January 2022, roughly 680 of these were T-64 variants.[81]

Interestingly, in April 2022 the Czechoslovak Group, comprising arms companies in both Czechia and Slovakia, agreed to repair Ukrainian 'Soviet-era' T-64s.[82] A contract was also signed between the Czech state-owned VOP CZ company and Ukraine's Ukroboronprom state defence conglomerate for T-64 repair.[83] The Polish tank manufacturer Bumar-Łabędy also signed an agreement with Ukroboronprom to repair Ukrainian T-64s in April 2023.[84] Given that both Czechoslovakia and Poland neither built nor used the T-64 during the Cold War, it will be interesting to know how they will conduct repairs on the Ukrainian T-64s since it has little commonality with the T-72s that these countries produced and used. It is likely that they will also be tasked with refurbishing the many T-64s that Ukraine still has in storage which it currently lacks the capacity to overhaul.

Ukrainian T-64BV of the 17th 'Kostiantyn Pestushko' Tank Brigade destroyed by an ATGM near Troitske, Luhansk in February 2015. The entire crew (commander Sergeant Major Alexey Ostashevkiy, gunner Sergeant Major Konstantin Tkachuk, and driver Private First Class Vasiliy Denisyuk) were killed. Ukrainian T-64BVs have borne the brunt of the tank fighting throughout the Russo–Ukrainian War and suffered losses accordingly. (LostArmour)

AUTOLOADERS & FLYING TURRETS

Soviet autoloaders have been subjects of myths and misunderstandings since the Cold War. One particular myth commonly seen in older books is that the autoloaders have a propensity to 'eat' carelessly placed limbs. Setting aside the fact that no one has ever produced a confirmed case of this happening despite T-72s being in use with many different countries for nearly half a century, there are protective panels designed to prevent this. They can be removed to gain access to the autoloader space, but in that event, the autoloader is no different from any other piece of heavy machinery. Simple common sense and proper training should be enough to ensure that fantastical scenarios like 'snagging clothes and ramming the arm into the breech' do not occur.

The autoloader has also been widely blamed for the notorious 'turret-tossing' phenomenon, where the detonation of the ammo conveyor/carousel sends the turret flying in a spectacular explosion. It is important to remember that the T-64/72/80 family are fundamentally 1960s tank designs: at the time, the best way to protect a tank's ammunition was thought to be storing it below the turret ring. This was because the main threat to tanks then were direct-fire weapons such as tanks or other AT weapons, usually aimed at a target's centre-of-mass, which happens to be around the turret ring. In practice, a tank's hull is often obscured by obstacles or terrain, thus shifting the aim-point upwards towards the turret.

In this respect, the T-72's carousel has a slight edge over the T-64/80's conveyor since the former's horizontally stacked charges, which are more vulnerable to being ignited or detonated if hit than the projectiles, are lower than the vertical ones in the latter. However, the carousel has a lower capacity than the conveyor, and to compensate there is more loose stowage within the turret of a T-72. This effectively negates the reduced risk from the lower carousel, and thus the crew must choose between having more ammunition or potentially greater survivability if hit.

Modern Western MBTs have adopted blow-out panels, which vent the explosion outwards if the ammunition is detonated or ignited. It is worth noting, though, that almost all of them only use blow-out panels for the *turret* ammunition and *not* for the hull. If they are penetrated in the hull and the ammunition is detonated, the result would not be very different from a T-64/72/80. The only exception is the American M1 Abrams, where all ammunition is stored within compartments with blow-out panels.

T-64B (top) and T-72 (bottom) ammunition stowage diagrams from Soviet training posters. The T-80's stowage is similar to the T-64's. Particularly noteworthy on the T-72 are the two brown charges stacked horizontally above the carousel: these are slotted under the commander and gunner's legs when they are seated in the tank! (Author's collection)

The spectacular explosion of a Russian T-72B3 near Novoazovsk, captured in May 2022 by a Chinese news crew. The turret and gun (six metres long) can be seen flying to a considerable height. It later inspired the cover art of a Trumpeter T-72B3 model kit. (Phoenix TV)

RELIABILITY

Reliability is an incredibly important quality that is often neglected and oversimplified: in most books on tanks (or any weapon system), it is often vaguely summarised as 'X was reliable' or 'unreliable' etc. However, tank reliability is a complex topic, as well as heavily context-dependent on things like crew training, operating environment, and manufacturing quality, among other things. Nowhere can this be better illustrated than with the T-64. One will often come across this narrative that the T-64 was unreliable, over-complicated, and broke down frequently, especially in the memoirs published by UVZ or from supporters of the T-72 like Murakhovsky and Kostenko, usually backed up by anecdata or testimonies.[85] Conversely, there are others like Saenko and Suvorov who present their own views that the T-64 was a fine enough weapon once it matured and crew training improved, and these will be backed by their own anecdata and testimonies.[86]

Anecdata can be useful sources of information, but are not enough on their own to really give a reasonable picture of reliability. It is helpful to at least have some quantitative basis for measuring reliability; in Soviet tank literature this was generally given by the failure parameter ω, which represents the number of failures (i.e. faults that prevent a tank from completing its mission) per 1,000km, calculated based on test data. In general, the Soviet military required a tank to have $\omega \leq 1$ (i.e. no more than one failure per 1,000km) before overhaul and $\omega \leq 0.8$ up to the warranty period.[87] To put things into perspective, the first prototype T-64As and T-72s had $\omega = 15$ and $\omega = 9$, respectively.[88]

The Soviets conducted fairly extensive tests in 'controlled military operations' (i.e. following military operating guidelines) between 1983–1984 to determine the reliability of their three MBT types, the T-64, T-72, and T-80.[89] These results were published in 1986 and can be summarised in a 1987 graph of ω for all three MBTs vs. year of manufacture.[90] They show that the T-64 had the lowest failure rate by 1979, i.e. it was the most reliable among the three and the only one that met the $\omega \leq 1$ condition at the time! This should not be too surprising, as even by 1973 the T-64 had already met it, and the rise in the failure rate can mostly be attributed to the introduction of the new *Ob* FCS and *Kobra* complex in 1976, as annotated in the graph.

The results article also provides the durability indicators for the engines and running gear of the three tanks.[91] There are two metrics used: R_{90} and R_{sr}. The former gives the component's lifetime on 90 percent of the tanks tested, while the latter is the lifetime averaged across all tanks tested. In general, R_{90} is the more consistent indicator, since R_{sr} can be skewed by long-lived outliers, hence the former is given here. The data shows that the T-64's 5TDF engine (300 hours) was somewhat less durable in service than the T-72's V-46 engine (320 hours), but not by a large margin, especially considering the V-46 was a more mature design. The T-80's GTD-1000 gas turbine engine fared very poorly by comparison (160 hours).

There is a little bit more to the story: during comparative trials in 1979 (by which time the T-64A and T-72 had been in service for six and four years, respectively), the T-64A's 5TDF had $\omega = 1.87$ while the T-72's V-46-6 had $\omega = 1.97$. However, the 5TDF was also being tested with the then-experimental autonomous flare heating system, and excluding its failures, the 5TDF had $\omega = 0.78$. In particular, the V-46-6 suffered from serious quality control problems and design defects, while the 5TDF did not have a single failure from those causes.[92]

The T-64's transmission, road wheels, tracks, and drive wheels all outperformed both the T-72 and T-80's equivalents in terms of R_{90} even though the R_{sr} is lower. For example, the T-64's reputedly 'fragile' road wheels had a R_{90} lifetime of 5,900km, exceeding the T-72 (5,500km) and T-80 (3,200km).[93] Chobitok attributes this to better design and manufacturing for the T-64, while the T-72 and T-80's components were overbuilt and suffered from poor quality control, leading to inconsistent durability.[94]

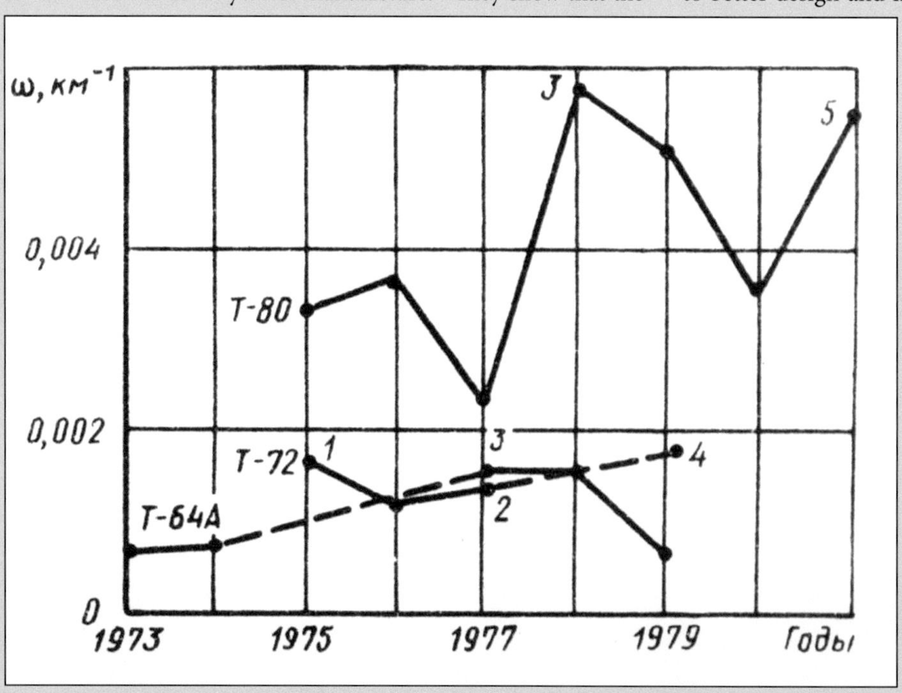

Graph of ω vs. year of manufacture for the three MBT types. Dashed lines indicate extrapolation due to no tanks tested from those years. The numbers represent milestones: (1) T-72 mass production begins, (2) V-46-6 engine installed in T-72, (3) *Kobra* weapons complex introduced in T-64 and T-80, (4) TPD-K1 installed in T-72, and (5) GTD-1000TF engine installed in T-80. (Razvalov, 1987)

The T-64's short torsion bars did initially prove less durable than conventional ones like those of the T-72 due to imperfect manufacturing processes. However, a 1985 study of the various torsion bar types used by Soviet tanks showed that the torsion bars used by the T-64 were more durable than those on the T-72 or T-80 (79 percent of T-64 bars tested survived 500,000 cycles, vs. 57 percent and 59 percent for the T-72 and T-80, respectively).[95] Furthermore, thanks to the small road wheels and long torsion keys, the torsion bars of the T-64 can be replaced without removing the road wheels or torsion keys.[96]

The T-64 also has a reputation for being difficult to maintain compared to the T-72 or T-80. Looking at the maintenance manuals for both the T-64B and the T-80B, this seems to be the case: daily maintenance tasks are scheduled to take two hours on a T-64B and only 1–1.5 hours on a T-80B. The T-72 also has it easier: based on a poster describing the maintenance tasks, it also takes 1.2–1.5 hours. End of story? Not quite.

Consider these test results published in 1987, where three tank companies composed of T-80Bs, T-72As, and T-64Bs were tested in long-distance marches, with daily 300km marches and three hours of daily maintenance over several days. As expected, the T-64B required the most effort for its daily maintenance (5.5 man-hours), the T-80B requiring only four man-hours and T-72A the least at 3.3 man-hours. However, the T-64B ends up having a much greater average mileage between a failure and a previously detected and fixed defect (739km) compared to the other two (T-80B: 517km; T-72A: 410km). It was also assessed to have a lower probability of undetected defects causing a failure in the next day.[97]

Why is this? The answer is relatively straightforward, according to Chobitok: the T-64B's designers were more realistic when it came to describing the required daily maintenance tasks. These had a higher chance of finding and fixing defects before they could cause the tank to fail. The lower service times in the T-72 and T-80B manuals look great on paper, but they are quite optimistic, and result in less thorough maintenance.[98]

1.2: T-72: Uralian Alternative

Russian T-72B *'Karavan'* of the Southern Military District in occupied territory, Zaporizhzhia *oblast*. Note the large road wheels, as well as the single-pin tracks characteristic of older T-72s (RIA)

As the Kharkov team under Morozov continued to work on improving the T-64 and ironing out its problems, it was realised that 5TDF production would be insufficient if war broke out and Soviet tank production had to be drastically increased. Thus, a cheaper and simpler 'mobilisation' tank was needed: both KhKBM and UKBTM were tasked with adapting the T-64 to take a more conventional V-12 diesel engine. Every Soviet tank since the T-34 had used a V-12 diesel engine, so this engine type was reasonably mature and, most importantly, cheap. KhKBM successfully adapted and tested the V-45 diesel engine on the Object 439, and this was originally the preferred 'mobilisation' tank.

However, UVZ and UKBTM had no desire to work on a rival's product, in favour of their 'own' design, the Object 172M. UKBTM's original Object 172 was, for all intents and purposes, a T-64A with a stretched engine compartment designed to take a V-12 diesel engine instead of the 5TDF and a new autoloader. However, UKBTM, led by Valeriy Venediktov after Kartsev moved to Moscow in 1969, was not satisfied with merely modifying a product of their Kharkovite rivals and decided that they could do better. They began to introduce more and more changes, and these resulted in the Object 172M, which was adopted as the T-72 *Ural* medium tank in 1975.

It is commonly stated that one of the reasons the T-72 was put into production is that it was cheaper than the T-64, but this is not strictly true. In the British comedy/documentary 'Yes, Minister', one of the 'three articles of civil service faith' is 'it's more expensive to do things cheaply': the T-72A actually cost about 30 percent more than a contemporary T-64A.[99] Entirely new production lines and tooling had to be set up to build the T-72 and its spare parts, which of course needed even more money. Nevertheless, to put a long story short, UVZ had some fairly powerful friends in the Soviet military and political hierarchy, and they secured the T-72's future in production.[100] The T-72A and T-72B are indeed cheaper than the T-64B, but that is because they use significantly more primitive FCSs compared to the T-64B.

Soviet-era T-72s can be roughly divided into three categories:

- T-72 *Ural* (Object 172M): Original production model with cast steel turret and coincidence rangefinder.
- T-72A (Object 176): Cast '*Kvartz*' turret with moulding material left in a cavity as a form of composite armour. TPD-K1 laser rangefinder/sight on most tanks.
- T-72B (Object 184): Significantly improved armour with ERA, characteristic enlarged turret with undercuts. 1A40 FCS.

There are also the export/Warsaw Pact licence-built T-72M and T-72M1 models, which roughly correspond to the original T-72 and T-72A, respectively, with some minor differences. In general, the basic T-72 *Ural* and T-72M are obsolete and not used in large numbers by either Russia or Ukraine at the time of writing. Thus, this section will focus on the T-72A/M1 and T-72B variants.

As the T-72 is fairly well-known in the West, this section will not go into too much depth about the T-72 beyond the features that distinguish it from the T-64 and T-80. It will mostly serve to provide background for the modernised T-90 and T-72B3, which will be covered separately under Russian post-Soviet tanks. The author regrets not having the space to go into too much depth on the panoply of T-72 variants.

This Russian T-72, seen in May 2023, is a very rare specimen: one of the first T-72 *Urals*, with a coincidence rangefinder and the IR searchlight mounted on the left of the turret, instead of on the right for later T-72s. It has been fitted with *Kontakt*-1 ERA in an improvised manner, as well as the customary 'BBQ grill' turret roof protection. (Sini Otechestva)

T-72s of the Eastern Military District assembled for the opening ceremony of the *Vostok* 2018 exercise. A T-72AV leads the column, followed by a T-72B1 and other T-72Bs. Note the different ERA configurations. (Mil.ru)

Firepower

T-72B of the Western Military District firing during qualifiers for the annual Russian Tank Biathlon in 2019. (Mil.ru)

Early T-72As use the 125mm 2A46 main gun, while the T-72B and late production T-72As have the improved 2A46M. The T-72 family has a different main gun mounting to that of the T-64 and T-80 due to the changed autoloader, which means that the guns are not completely interchangeable between the two tank families. Main guns intended for the T-64/T-80 families have different GRAU indices (2A26M, 2A46-1, 2A46-2, 2A46M-1, 2A46M-4) to those of the T-72 family (2A26M-2, 2A46, 2A46M, 2A46M-5) to avoid confusion.[101] They are otherwise ballistically identical and use the same ammunition.

The primary firepower differences between the T-72 and the T-64/T-80 families lie in the autoloader and FCS. T-72s use a completely different electrically powered autoloader mechanism, known generically as the 'AZ' (*avtomat zaryazhaniya* — 'automatic loader') to distinguish it from the T-64/T-80's MZ. There are two different AZ models found in Soviet-era T-72s: the AZ-172 in the T-72, T-72M, T-72A, T-72B1, and T-72M1, and the AZ-184 in the T-72B. The latter is modified to handle GLATGMs such as the 9M119 *Refleks*. The projectiles and charges in the AZ are stacked horizontally in cassettes arranged radially within the carousel at the floor of the fighting compartment, with charges on top; Kartsev did not like the vertically stowed charges in the T-64 isolating the driver from the fighting compartment.[102] It also reduces the size of the carousel when viewed from the side or front, making it more difficult to hit from those angles. The trade-off is that the T-72's AZ autoloader can only hold 22 rounds compared to 28 in the MZ autoloader. To compensate for this, the T-72A carries 22 extra rounds (23 in the T-72B) in the fighting compartment and next to the driver.[103] Manual loading is also significantly harder with the AZ in the event of an electrical systems failure or malfunction than with the MZ and requires the cooperation of both the gunner and commander.[104]

As with the original MZ conveyor, the AZ's carousel can only rotate in one direction (counterclockwise). It is often mentioned that the AZ autoloader rotates faster than the MZ, but according to Saenko the devil is in the details: the manual says '*up to* 70°/s' while the MZ is rated at 26°/second, but the electric drive takes time to accelerate and is also affected by the presence of other shells in the carousel. The T-72 manual does not give the loading time with a full carousel rotation, so Saenko decided to measure it himself. He found it took around 20 seconds with an empty carousel, and up to 28 seconds with a loaded carousel. The hydraulic MZ takes 19.5 seconds.[105]

As on the T-64, either the gunner or commander may select the round before pressing the load button. There is no 'series' mode for the AZ autoloaders; the gunner/commander must press the load button each time. For reasons known only to the T-72's designers, the AZ ammo counter is located on the gunner's side instead of the commander's side. This means the commander can easily lose track of how much ammunition he has of each type. Dominikanets also claims the counter is 'disgusting', often breaking down and lying about the ammo in the AZ. It will also only show the amount for one type of ammunition at a time, unlike the MZ.[106]

The spent charge stub ejection mechanism is inherited from the T-62. On the T-62, this system was a necessity because of the large spent shell casings, but the utility of this system in the T-72 is debatable: it does help reduce the build-up of fumes from the spent case stub after firing, but others such as SR have derided it as an unnecessary complication. If there is a power failure, and the catcher/ejector is stuck in the intermediate or upper position, it is impossible to fire the gun because the stub ejected from the gun can pose a hazard. There is no provision to manually lower it into the proper position in such a scenario, unlike on the T-62.[107]

The original T-72 *Ural* used the TPD-2-49 coincidence rangefinder, as on the T-64A. This was soon replaced by the TPD-K1 with integrated laser rangefinder and independent vertical stabilisation as the gunner's primary sight, married to the 2E28M *Siren* ('Lilac') two-plane stabiliser. Many older T-72s were retrofitted with the TPD-K1, since it was designed to fit into the TPD-2-49's housing, and it is also the standard sight on export T-72M/M1 models. The TPD-K1 adjusts the reticle based on range data and shot ballistics: the gunner must re-lay the reticle on-target and manually compensate for lead. As such, it is not a 'true' FCS like the *Ob*.[108] The gunner also has his own forward periscope to use in addition to the

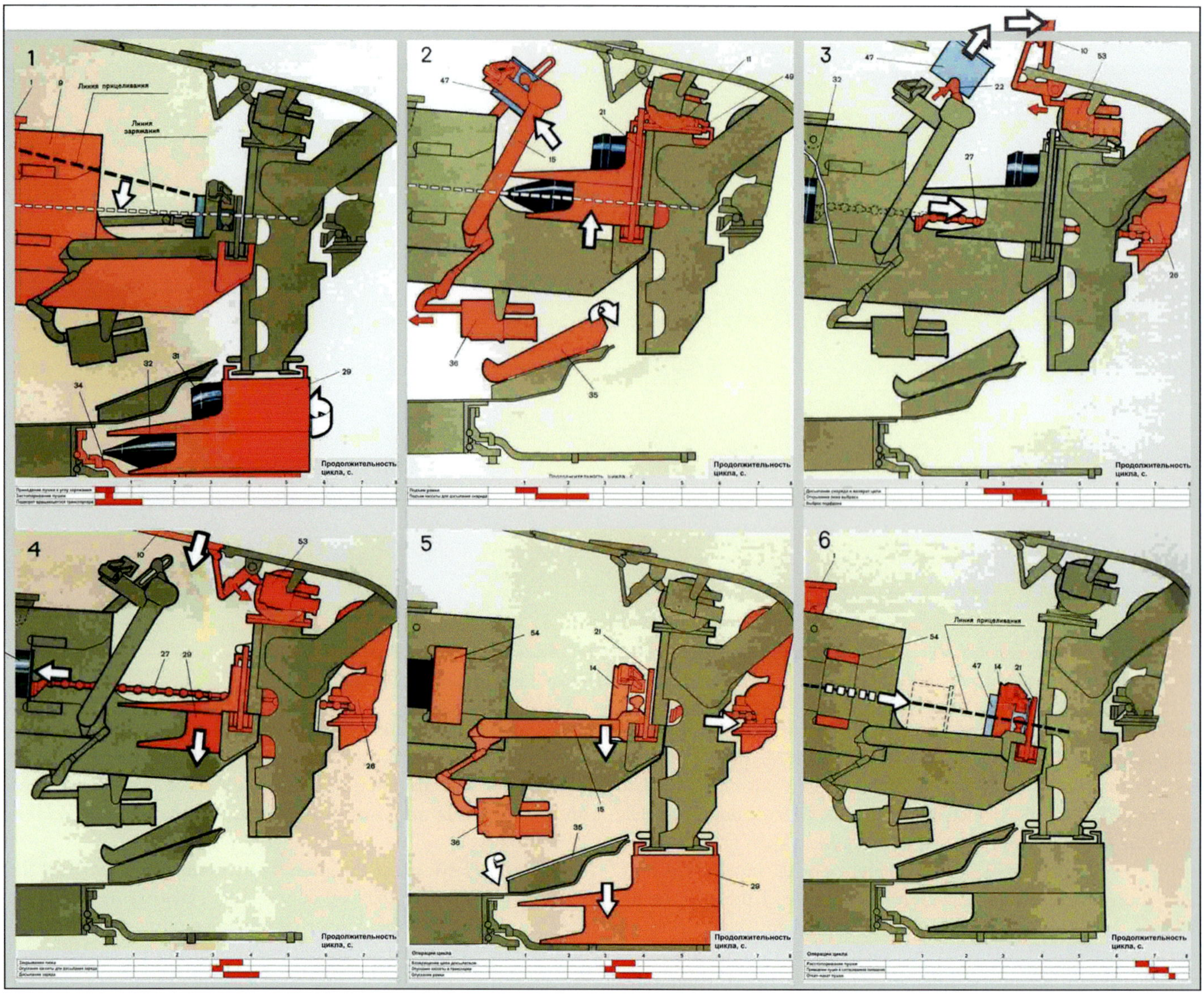

Soviet training poster illustration of the AZ's loading cycle. The entire process takes 7.5 seconds, according to the cyclogram at the bottom of each picture. (Author's collection)

sight: this compensates for the TPD-K1's fixed magnification and, according to Dominikanets, makes it easier for the gunner to find his target.

In the 1980s, the TPD-K1 was modernised with the addition of a 'lateral lead generation device' (*ustroystva virabotki bovovikh uprezhdeniy*, UVBU) to calculate the necessary lead amount as the gunner tracks a moving target. This is displayed as a number in the sight, and the gunner must then compensate for it manually using the sight's lead scale markings.[109] Together with the 2E42-2 *Zhasmin* ('Jasmine') two-plane stabiliser and the gunner's 1K13 night/auxiliary sight, the entire T-72B FCS is designated 1A40-1. It is an improvement over the TPD-K1, but still considerably inferior to the *Ob* FCS on the T-64B/80B.

The 1K13 is also a part of the 9K120 *Svir* GLATGM complex. The *Svir* complex allows the T-72B to fire the 9M119 *Refleks* GLATGM, a laser beam-riding SACLOS missile that receives command signals via the pulses of the laser beam emitted by the 1K13 sight. This is a simpler and more reliable GLATGM system than the radio-command *Kobra*, but the weaker laser of the 1K13 restricts the *Refleks* to a range of 4km when fired from a T-72B. The T-72B1 (*Object* 184-1) does not use the 1K13 and thus lacks GLATGM capability; it has the TPN-1-49-23 or improved TPN-3-49 *Kristall-PA* night sight instead, as does the T-72A.

Unlike on the T-64, the T-72's ZU-72 mounting for the *Utyos* AAMG is manually operated, forcing the commander to expose himself out of the cupola in order to use the *Utyos.*[110] Syrian and Russian T-72 crews operating in urban environments are almost never observed using the *Utyos* because it is almost suicidal for the commander. Furthermore, the cupola must be turned backwards first in order to use the *Utyos* against targets ahead of the T-72 because the cupola's OU-3GK IR searchlight blocks the machine gun when the cupola faces forwards.

The T-72's commander uses the TKN-3M primary day/night sight. This can be distinguished from the T-64's TKN-3VM by the handles on each side of the device. It is difficult for the commander to observe his surroundings when the tank is moving or standing on a slope since he must move the cupola with the TKN-3M's handles and 'elbow grease' and there is no stabilisation. The cupola will also not automatically counter-rotate if the turret is traversed: the commander must press a button on the right handle of the TKN-3M, which will link the cupola to the turret ring and fix it as the turret rotates. The button on the left handle is the commander's turret traverse override. As on the T-64, the commander does not have elevation controls, and thus cannot lay the gun himself. There are four other periscopes on his cupola, which provide a better overall field of view than the T-64B's cupola.

The 1A40-1 FCS of the T-72B. The UVBU is the black scope next to the main orange one. T-72B1s and T-72As that lack the *Svir* GLATGM complex use the 1A40 instead.

A DNR T-72B tank commander handles the *Utyos* AAMG. It is fitted to the ZU-72 mounting on a separate ring to the commander's cupola, fed by 60-round boxes. (Dialog.ua)

Protection

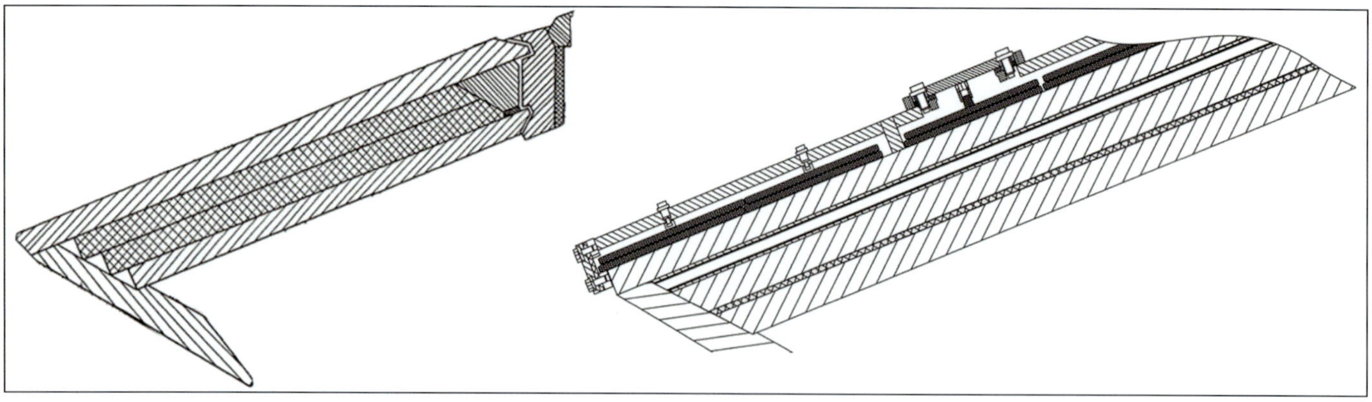

T-72 upper glacis armour configurations: early T-72A and T-72M1 ('60-105-50', left), late T-72B with reflecting plates and *Kontakt*-5 (right). (Andrei Tarasenko)

T-72As and T-72M1s use a similar upper glacis composite armour layout to the T-64A, but with a difference: the front plate was thinned down to 60mm and the back plate thickened to 50mm, while the STB fibreglass layers remained unchanged ('60-105-50'). As a result of the *Otrazhenie* programme, existing tanks received a 16mm applique plate on the upper glacis in 1983.[111] T-72As and T-72M1s also use the so-called *Kvartz* ('Quartz') turret.[112] It derives its name from the sintered quartz sand (essentially a ceramic block) used as a casting mould and simply left inside the T-72's turret as a form of composite armour.[113] This has improved resistance against shaped charges compared to the original T-72's monolithic cast steel turret. It is thicker than the contemporary ceramic-sphere turret of late production T-64s but simpler to produce, an important consideration for mass production.

In the late 1970s and early 1980s, T-72As began switching to spaced armour upper glacis layouts, dispensing with the fibreglass layers.[114] On early T-72Bs, the RHA plates were once again retained, but in between were two 10mm and two 20mm HHA plates, each separated by 10mm air spaces. This increased the upper glacis' mass by about 20 percent, but yielded a significant increase in protection against kinetic penetrators: in tests, it proved capable of stopping the 125mm 3BM32 *Vant* depleted uranium APFSDS, even when increased propellant was used.[115] The installation of *Kontakt*-1 ERA, which came as standard on the T-72B, rendered the glacis impenetrable to any non-tandem-charge weapon in the 1980s.

The T-72B also introduced a new turret design that used what are known as 'reflecting plates' (*otrzhayushchimi listami*). This is essentially a non-explosive reactive armour (NERA) package, with the turret front containing two large cavities. Each cavity has an array of twenty 30mm blocks, each consisting of three layers bonded together: 21mm armour plate, 6mm rubber, and 3mm metal 'reflecting plate'. Three separators are welded to the armour plate of each block, providing an inter-block separation of 22mm. Both cavities have an additional 45mm armour plate between the 'reflecting plates' and the inner wall of the cavity. This required a significantly enlarged turret front in order to accommodate the plates, hence the characteristic 'bulged' turret shape with undercuts.[116]

Cutaway of a T-72M1's *Kvartz* turret: the cast steel has rusted, while the sintered quartz block inside remains grey. The T-72A's turret composite configuration is identical. (Tank-Net)

A rather bare Russian T-72B sighted during the first days of the 2022 invasion. It has not been fitted with *Kontakt*-1 ERA, the IR searchlight, smoke grenade launchers, or a thermal sleeve, possibly fresh from storage. Note the distinctive undercuts of the T-72B's reflecting plate turret. (TASS)

As the name might suggest, 'reflecting plates' work using the reflection of shockwaves at the boundary between the rubber and armour plate induced by a shaped charge's jet to cause the rubber and 'reflecting plate' to bulge outwards, propelled by the energy transfer of the shockwaves. The bulging plate disrupts the jet and degrades its penetration. Against kinetic projectiles, the reflecting plates act as a spaced armour array, since the thin bulging plates do not significantly affect such penetrators. Nevertheless, during testing, the reflecting plate sections of the T-72B turret withstood hits from the 125mm 3BM26 tungsten-cored APFSDS.[117] The reflecting plate turret armour is relatively easy to manufacture as well as replace following combat damage: simply cutting open the welded cavity roof section and replacing damaged plates while patching any holes in the cast steel will restore the turret to its full integrity. This is impossible to do for either the T-72 *Kvartz* or T-64 ceramic-sphere turrets.

From 1987, reflecting plates were used for the upper glacis; however, detailed information is lacking on the exact armour scheme.[118] Based on drawing measurements and descriptions, the armour layout is thought to be 50mm front RHA plate, followed by a 35mm air space, and two 60mm RHA plates separated by a 10mm anti-radiation lining. The 3mm 'reflecting plates' are attached by a 6mm rubber layer to the rear and front faces of the 50mm and 60mm plates, respectively.

Many T-72As have been upgraded with *Kontakt*-1 ERA, receiving the designation T-72AV in Soviet service. The T-72AV package consisted of 219 blocks: 61 on the turret front, 62 on the hull front, and 96 on the side-skirts, and it weighs about 1.4 tonnes. The latter are attached directly to the side-skirts, instead of on frames like the T-64BV, which saves weight but also means they fall off more easily, while the turret uses a different arrangement to the T-64BV's for slightly better coverage (73 percent and 62 percent of the hull front and turret, respectively).[119]

The T-72B was designed with ERA from the start, hence why there is no 'T-72BV'. Initially, this was the *Kontakt*-1 ERA package, consisting of 227 blocks: 61 on the frontal hull, 70 on the turret, and 96 on the side-skirts.[120] Instead of being mounted on V-shaped frames like on the T-64BV and T-72AV, the *Kontakt*-1 blocks on the T-72B were attached directly to the turret: it is not known exactly why, because *Kontakt*-1 works best when hit at an oblique angle and mounting it this way significantly reduces its effectiveness. It is possible that the better coverage achieved with this method was considered an acceptable trade-off, given that the T-72B 'reflecting plate' turret has stronger base protection than either the T-72AV or T-64BV turrets.

From 1988, T-72Bs received the *Kontakt*-5 ERA package, consisting of eight blocks on the turret front, 12 on the upper glacis, three on each side-skirt, and 21 smaller blocks on the turret roof.[121] Each block can contain multiple 4S22 explosive elements, resulting in a total of 360 elements.[122] This significantly improved their protection: US Army tests of T-72Bs with *Kontakt*-5 showed that they were effectively impenetrable to standard NATO AT weapons of the 1980s.[123] However, the *Kontakt*-5 package, which also weighs 1.5 tonnes, only covers about 50 percent of the T-72B's turret front. The hull is better covered, resulting in total frontal coverage of at least 55 percent.

T-72s have the usual 902B *Tucha*-1 smoke grenade launching system, built-in dozer blade, and engine smoke-laying system. However, for reasons known only to the T-72's designers, the *Tucha* controls are on the gunner's side instead of the commander's side, as on the T-64 or T-80. This means that the commander has to tell the gunner to launch the smoke grenades instead of doing it himself, which can waste valuable time and distracts the gunner from his duties.

Russian T-72B with *Kontakt*-5 ERA. It is often known as the '1989 model' (even though it first appeared in 1988) or 'T-72BM', but officially it is simply a T-72B. The side-skirt ERA is not mounted here. It has the 1K13 sight, allowing it to fire the *Refleks* GLATGM, as well as mine ploughs. Note also the depressions over the turret front, which can be cut open to replace the reflecting plates mounted inside if damaged. (Denis Mokrushin)

Mobility

In general, the T-72 family is a lot more conservative in terms of their automotive design features. The T-72A and T-72M1 use the 780hp V-46-6 liquid-cooled multi-fuel 12-cylinder V-12 four-stroke diesel engine. The T-72A weighs significantly more than the T-64A (41.5 tonnes vs. 38 tonnes), hence the extra horsepower was needed to maintain a similar power/weight ratio (18.8hp/t). The T-72B is even heavier (44.5 tonnes): it uses the boosted V-84 engine family providing 840hp and a slightly increased power/weight ratio (18.9hp/t). Both the T-72A and T-72B have significantly better acceleration characteristics than the underpowered T-64BV thanks to the higher power/weight ratio.

The V-46 and V-84 families share the same basic layout and operating features, and are interchangeable. Both are based on the V-2 diesel engine that powered the T-34, whose development can be traced back to the 1930s. As such, they are quite reliable, with production well mastered. They are also less demanding in terms of the fuel and maintenance quality and driver management, and also start more easily in cold weather than the 5TDF. Dominikanets says that with proper maintenance, a T-72B will reliably start at temperatures below -20 C even after a week's downtime.[124] This was improved on the V-84-1 with intake air heating.

In terms of fuel consumption, the T-72 is roughly comparable to the T-64. The T-72's various engines are all multi-fuel capable, and accept diesel, kerosene, petrol, or mixtures of these. The V-12 four-stroke engines are, however, significantly more efficient when it comes to lubricant oil consumption, since they do not burn the oil with the fuel during combustion.

One thing the T-72 did keep from the T-64 was the BKP transmission units. The V-12 diesel engines were not designed for the BKP units, unlike the 5TDF, therefore an input gearbox ('guitar') is needed to attach the engine crankshaft to the shaft connecting the BKPs on each side, complicating access and maintenance. They are thus not interchangeable with the T-64's BKPs. The T-72 also uses a cooling fan for the engine radiator, unlike the T-64. These factors, combined with the larger size of the V-12 engines, result in a significantly larger engine compartment, which in turn contributes to the T-72's greater weight.

The driver controls and instruments are almost identical between contemporary T-64 and T-72 models: a driver-mechanic trained on one can easily drive the other with little to no retraining required. In contrast to the T-64, however, replacing the engine and transmission in a T-72 is significantly harder. It requires 94 man-hours of labour or 24 hours for a four-man maintenance team (almost double the T-64) to replace the engine, according to the manual.[125] Dominikanets notes that access to the various filters on the T-72B's engine is more difficult than in the T-64, which makes it harder to maintain.[126]

On the other hand, the T-72 is more 'idiotproof' than the T-64 and more forgiving of mistakes in handling and maintenance. Consider, for example, the cassette air filter on the T-72: anyone would understand that if the cassette becomes clogged with dust then it is time to clean it before the engine gets damaged. On the T-64's cassetteless air cleaner, this is not so obvious. The advantage this 'idiotproofness' confers is not trivial when one considers the level of education and training of Soviet army personnel, who

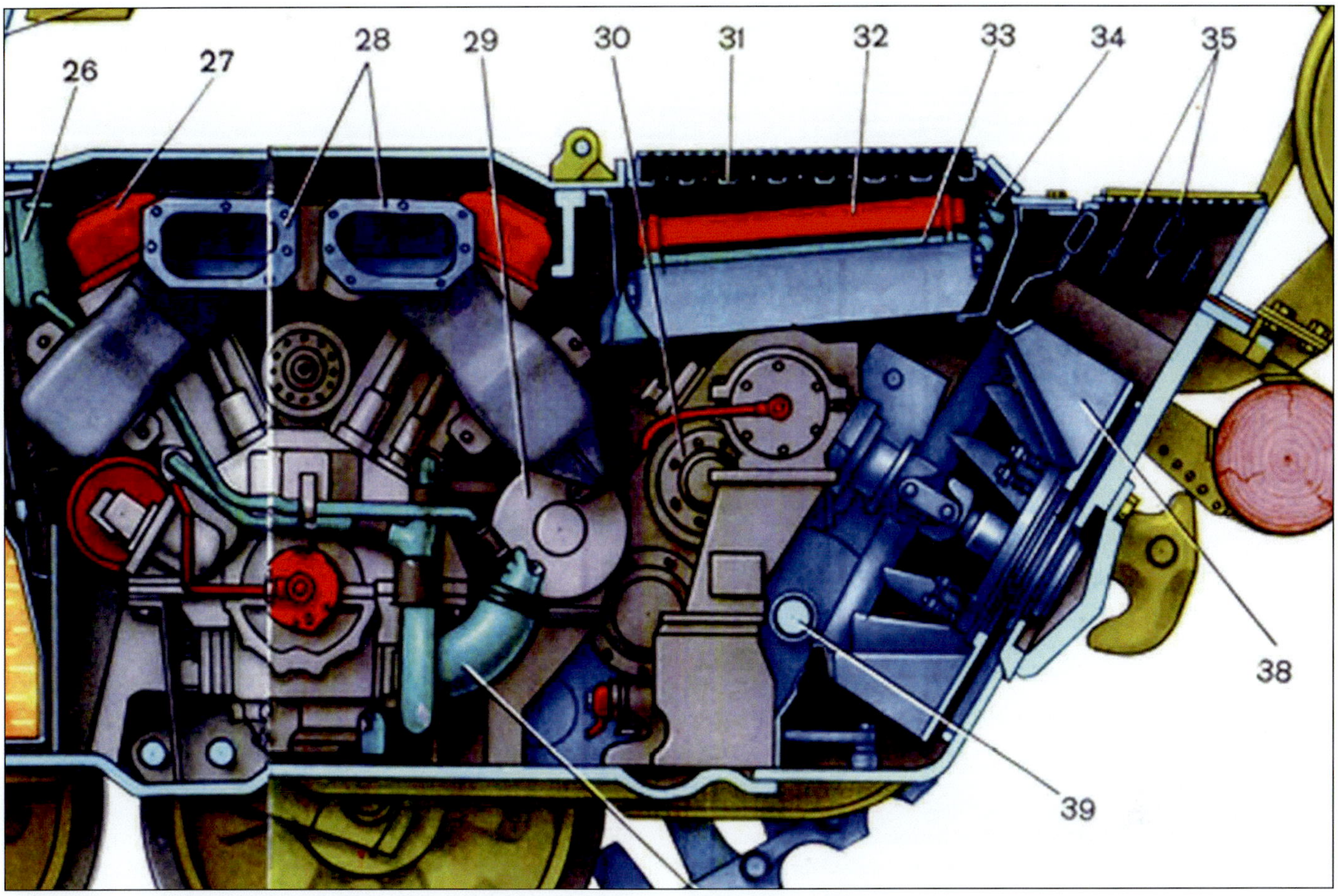

Cross-section of a T-72's engine compartment from a Soviet technical poster. The larger V-12 engine, transmission, and cooling fan (blue) result in a significantly longer engine compartment than the T-64's. (Author's collection)

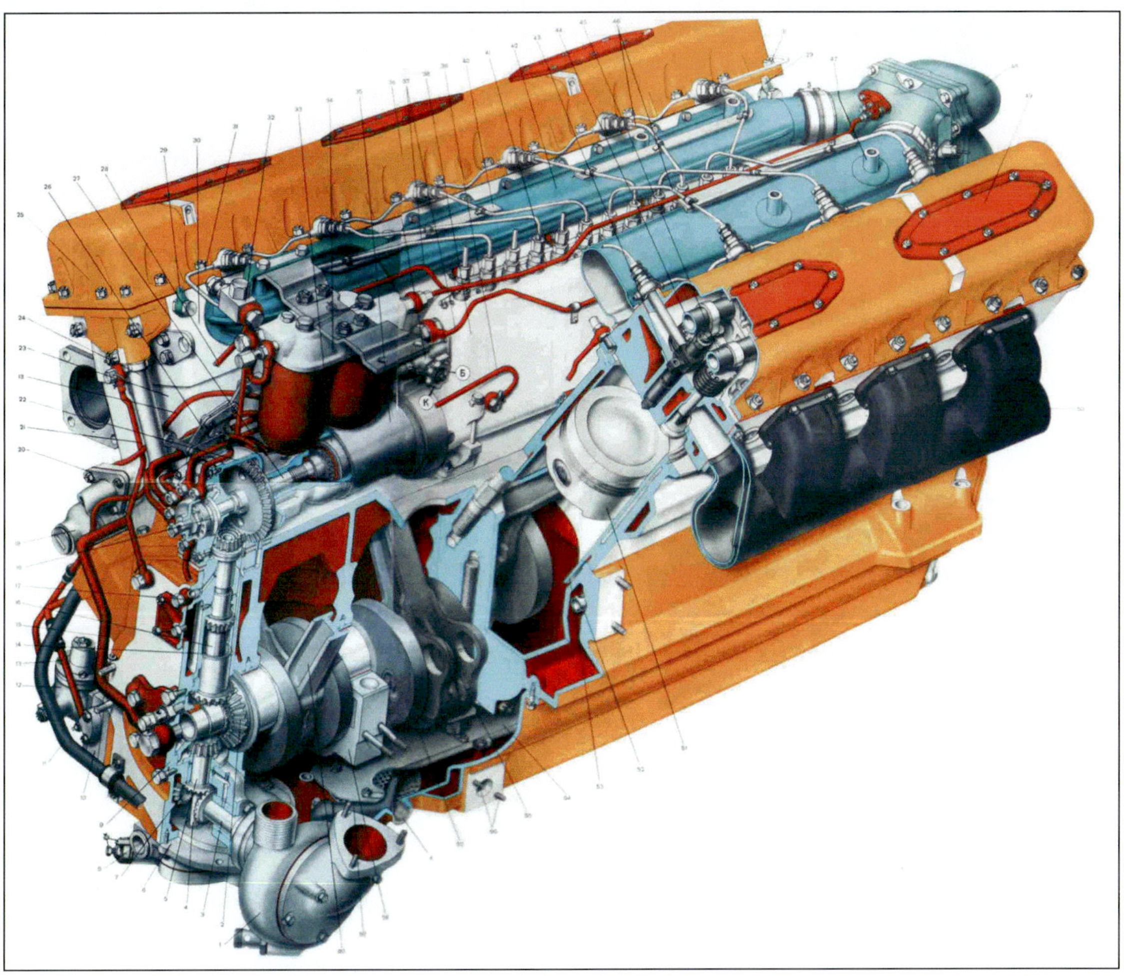

The V-84-1 840hp V-12 engine. A proven design, it is safe to say that the V-84 and related V-46 and V-92 power most of the tanks currently fighting in Ukraine. (Author's collection)

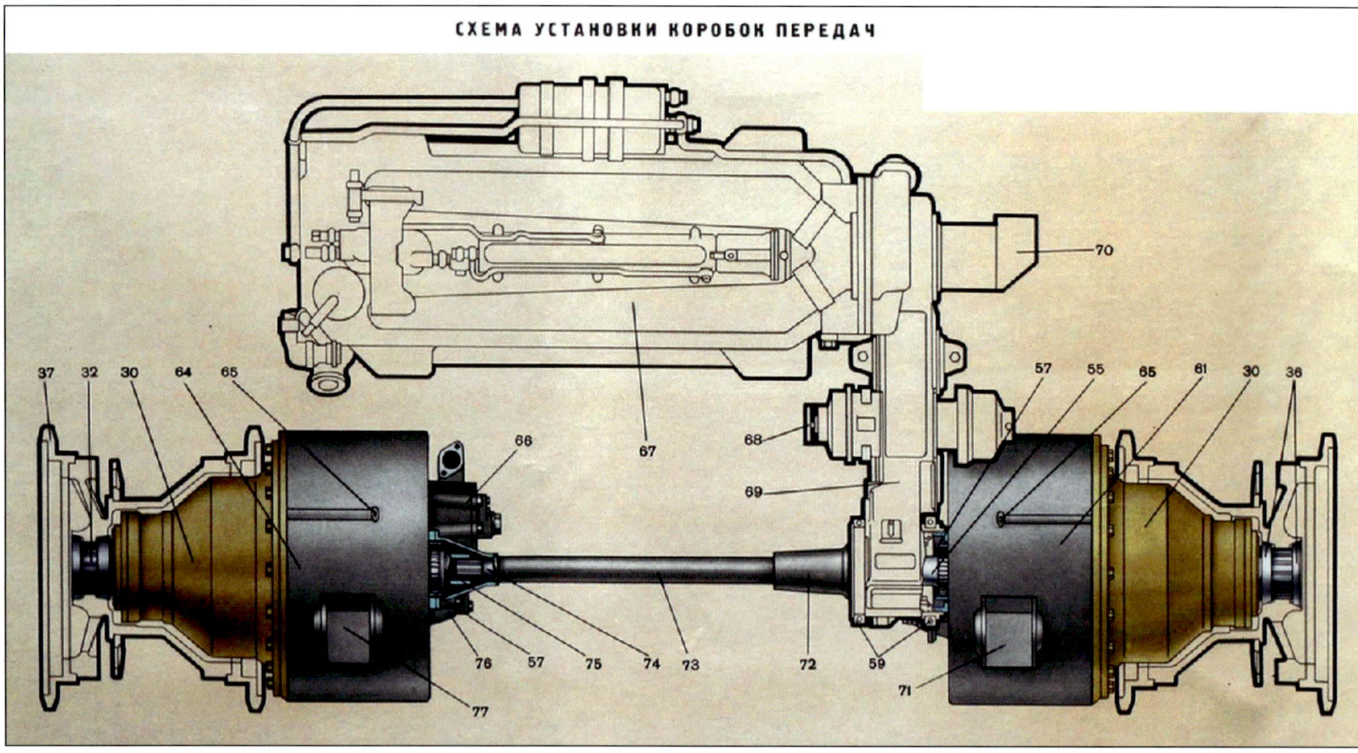

T-72 transmission scheme from a Soviet maintenance poster. While the T-72 uses BKP units similar to the T-64's, they are not interchangeable. (Author's collection)

primarily consisted of conscripts. Unlike a professional army such as the US or British armies, Soviet conscripts only served for two years. This meant that the average level of training of a serving conscript at any one time was not that high, and the T-72 was arguably better suited for such personnel than the more sophisticated T-64 or T-80. It was also significantly easier for drivers trained on the T-55 or T-62 to transition to a T-72 due to their shared automotive lineage.

The T-72 suspension is also more conventional, having more in common with the T-55 and T-62. The rubber-rimmed road wheels are larger than the T-64's and are primarily made of stamped aluminium.[127] The first, second, and sixth road wheels are attached to vane hydraulic shock absorbers, similar to those used on earlier tanks but with a greater travel range. Conventional full-length transverse torsion bars are used, which meant the torsion bars did not have to withstand as much shear stress, but required the road wheels to be placed asymmetrically. The suspension dynamic travel (how much a road wheel could move vertically over a bump) is also greater than on earlier tanks, resulting in a smoother ride than on the T-55 or T-62.[128]

While the T-72's suspension was a significant improvement over the T-55 and T-62's, it had some disadvantages compared to the T-64's suspension. The large aluminium road wheels are heavier than the T-64's, and more power is wasted rotating them during movement.[129] It also means that they must be removed before the torsion bars can be accessed, a time-consuming procedure. Aluminium is also a relatively expensive strategic material that is also important in aircraft production. The external rubber rims were a major cause of failure for the T-72's suspension, especially as the tank gained more weight, leading to accelerated wear and destruction.[130] Finally, the T-72's use of 'stiffer' vane hydraulic stabilisers and short torsion keys, result in notably inferior ride smoothness to the T-64 and worse accuracy when firing on the move.[131]

T-72s originally used one-piece single-pin 'live' tracks inherited from late production T-55 and T-62 tanks. These tracks were cheaper than the T-64's dual-pin tracks (₽1,900 (T-64) vs. ₽1,500 (T-72), 1985 prices), but also less durable.[132] Dominikanets imaginatively describes them as 'disgusting' and 'behaving like a cow on ice' in mud.[133] The large road wheels tend to compress mud or wet soil

T-72 suspension with road wheels removed, showing the torsion keys and vane hydraulic shock absorbers. (Alexey Khlopotov)

This screenshot from SR's video illustrates one of the problems that the T-72's suspension encounters in mud or wet sand, even on a modernised tank with dual-pin tracks as shown. Wet sand, compressed by the road wheels, has built up around the drive wheel, causing its teeth to disengage from the tracks. (SR)

between them and the tracks, which lack the drainage holes of the T-64's dual-pin tracks. This in turn results in mud or wet sand building up on the tracks and drive wheel, which can cause the latter to disengage from the tracks, resulting in a loss of mobility or de-tracking.[134]

The T-72's single-pin tracks do, however, perform better and have more traction than the T-64's in dry sand: fortunate, given the T-72's popularity in the Middle East. Late production T-72Bs can also use the T-90's dual-pin tracks, which perform better in mud than the T-72's original tracks, but are more complex and expensive. Older T-72s cannot use these tracks, due to incompatible drive wheels. It is therefore still common to see T-72s in service with single-pin tracks to this day.

Context

Of the three late-Cold War Soviet MBTs, the T-72 is certainly the most prolific and best known in the West. T-72s have seen action in almost every major conflict that has occurred since the Iran–Iraq War of 1980, often on both sides of the conflicts. The Russo–Ukrainian War is no exception, and both Russia and Ukraine are using T-72s in large numbers; even the latest T-90M is essentially a very heavily modernised T-72 at its core, as will be seen later.

Comparing the contemporary T-72B and T-64BV, on paper both have the same firepower, with the T-72B having better base armour protection and a higher power/weight ratio. However, there are two substantial differences between the T-72 and T-64 that do not get captured by merely looking at specification tables within the context of the Russo–Ukrainian War.

The first, and arguably most important, difference is the degree of automation. This is most apparent when comparing the FCSs: the T-72B's 1A40 requires a lot more manual input and adjustments than the *Ob* of the T-64BV/T-80BV. Dominikanets, who has served on both T-64BVs and T-72Bs, claims that the *Ob* allows a T-64BV (or T-80BV) to fight dynamically against several T-72Bs at once, assuming crews of equal skill.[135] The T-72A and T-72M1 are even worse off in this respect, since their FCS is even more primitive than the T-72B's. This weakness was only fixed with the introduction of the 1A40-4 FCS on the upgraded T-72B3 in 2012. It can also be seen in the manually operated commander's cupola. Features like these increase the crew's workload and may reduce their performance.

The second is the T-72's poor performance on mud and soft soil. 'General Mud', the bane of the Wehrmacht's tanks in 1941, was to prove just as formidable an opponent for Russian T-72s during the first phase of the Russian invasion in the spring thaw of 2022. The muddy conditions often restricted them to predictable roads that are vulnerable to ambushes or caused them to get hopelessly stuck and abandoned by their crews. The most dramatic example of this was during the battle of Brovary in March 2022, when a column of T-72s and other vehicles of the 6th Guards Tank Regiment were ambushed by Ukrainian forces and tried to get off the M01 highway, but got bogged down by the mud and was soon pounded by UAS-supported artillery and ATGMs. This resulted in the loss of 17 tanks and reportedly the death of the regiment commander.[136]

On the other hand, the T-72 still has the same 125mm gun as the T-64 or T-80, hence it is just as capable in the infantry support role against softer targets, where the differences in the FCS are not as critical. Some Ukrainian tankers have also expressed their appreciation for the better armour protection of the T-72B in particular when compared to the T-80BV or T-64BV during interviews. Certainly, there have been successful Ukrainian tankers who use older T-72, such as Lieutenant Nazar Vernihora, whose T-72B ambushed a Russian column retreating from Nova Basan, Chernihiv in March 2022 and was credited with destroying three armoured personnel carriers and one tank.[137]

Following the end of the Cold War, Russia settled on the T-72 as its primary MBT since the T-80 and T-90 were unaffordable given

T-72M1 'Sokil' ('Falcon') of the Ukrainian 54th 'Hetman Ivan Mazepa' Mechanised Brigade assaulting a ChVK *Vagner* trench. The tank ran out of 125mm ammunition, since it only carried 22 rounds in order to minimise the risk of ammunition detonation if hit, so it resorted to crushing the infantry in the trench. At least one *Vagner* soldier was seen crushed by the 42-tonne tank in the drone footage. (Batalyion K-2 54 OMBr, YouTube)

the precarious state of the Russian economy. Many of the T-72s were modernised beginning in the late 1990s, but as late as September 2021, the VSRF still used large numbers of unmodernised Cold War-era T-72s: discounting the modernised T-72BAs and T-72B3s, the VSRF still had 805 legacy T-72A and T-72B tanks, representing nearly a third of the VSRF's 2,609-strong active tank fleet at that time.[138] These were primarily used by the units of the Central and Eastern VOs, since they generally have a lower priority when it comes to modernisation and re-equipment. Many more are kept in storage, but there is no way to really know how many of them can be reactivated and whether they will be able to replace the horrendous losses suffered by the Russian T-72 fleet so far.

The ZSU proper did not use T-72s in first-line units before the Russo–Ukrainian War, since its production was not based in Ukraine. Most were put into storage after independence or sold abroad for much needed liquidity. In December 2014, the ZSU began reactivating stored T-72s in order to replace combat losses and expand its tank fleet.[139] Ukraine has also initiated a modernisation programme for its T-72s, described in Part 2. Prior to February 2022, Ukrainian T-72s were primarily used by reserve ZSU units such as the 3rd 'Zaliznyi' Tank Brigade.

After the Russian full-scale invasion, Ukraine has also received at least 250 T-72M1s (including modernised T-72M1Rs, discussed separately) from Poland as aid.[140] These have been used to replace losses and equip newly created mechanised units. As the war continues, it is likely that T-72s will constitute a larger proportion of the Ukrainian tank fleet, as the T-64 fleet dwindles and Ukraine acquires more T-72s either via captures or as aid from the West's stocks. It is also easier for the ex-Warsaw Pact NATO countries such as Poland, Bulgaria, Czechia, and Slovakia to logistically support the T-72, since all four were engaged in licence production of the T-72 for both domestic and export use.

The LNR and DNR did not begin using T-72s until August 2014. As noted in the T-64 section, they tried to maintain the fiction that their tanks were captured from Ukrainian military bases and storage sites by using only T-64s, but there were insufficient serviceable T-64s in Russian storage, which forced the Russians to begin sending T-72s. They have since become the mainstay of DNR and LNR tank units. In addition to 'separatist' T-72s, the Russians began sending in regular VSRF units with T-72s to intervene in support of the wavering 'separatist' movement. Although Russia denies this, there is considerable evidence disproving their denials.[141]

DNR T-72B, taken around the time of the Battle of Debaltseve, 2015. T-72s formed the bulk of 'separatist' tank units prior to 2022. (TASS)

1.3: T-80: Turbine-powered Hot-rod

In 1966, the Soviets became aware of American plans to fit a 1,500hp gas turbine engine into their next-generation MBT, the joint German–American MBT-70. While the MBT-70 ended up using a diesel engine, factions in the Soviet hierarchy became convinced that they must also have their own gas turbine tank, most notably Ustinov. Leningrad had been the home of the defunct Soviet heavy tank programme, for which KB-3 had some experience developing tanks with gas turbines. Its former chief designer, the well-connected Zhosef Kotin, also became Deputy Minister of Defence for Tank Production in 1968. He actively lobbied for the Soviets to adopt a gas turbine tank, which would naturally be a product of his former workplace.

These factors, in combination with the aforementioned early problems of the T-64A's 5TDF engine, led to KB-3 under chief designer Nikolai Popov being tasked with designing a gas turbine-powered T-64A in 1968, over the objections of some like Minister of Defence Andrei Grechko. It was given the index Object 219. The first prototype 219 *sp.*1 retained the same suspension as the T-64A, but it was found that it could not withstand the higher dynamic loads due to the increased power of the GTD-1000 gas turbine engine. Instead of attempting to modify it, the next prototype 219 *sp.*2 used a completely new suspension with large rubber-rimmed road wheels. In this form, the Object 219 was accepted into service as the T-80 in 1976, becoming the first service tank in the world powered solely by a gas turbine.[142] It was quickly followed by the T-80B in 1978, which incorporated the T-64B's advanced gunnery features.

In general, there was more 'cross-pollination' between the Kharkov T-64 and Leningrad T-80 programmes than with the T-72 family. However, the T-80 cost a lot more: in 1976, a T-80 (₽480,000) cost over three times more than a T-64A (₽140,000).[143] By the early 1980s, the price disparity had reduced somewhat with mass production, but a T-80B still cost twice as much as a T-64B. Despite this, at that time, the gas turbine's supporters dominated the upper echelons of the Soviet political and military hierarchies, most notably the powerful Ustinov. They ensured the T-80's future, at least for the time being.

Eventually, the Soviets decided that they had to standardise on one MBT, and as long as Ustinov was around, it had to be a gas turbine-powered tank. This led to the merging of the Leningrad T-80 and Kharkov *Kedr* (Object 476) programmes into the *Olkha* ('Alder') programme, combining the hull and chassis of the former and the turret and weapon systems of the latter. The result was the 'advanced T-80' (*T-80 usovershenstvovanniy*) or Object 219A.[144] With additional improvements, it entered serial production as the T-80U (Object 219AS) in 1985, the most advanced MBT to serve before the Soviet Union's collapse. Such capability carried a high price tag: a T-80U cost nearly three times a T-72B (₽824,000 vs. ₽280,000).[145]

When it comes to Soviet legacy T-80s, there are essentially three 'generations':

- T-80 (Object 219): basically a T-64A with a gas turbine engine and new suspension.
- T-80B (Object 219R): upgraded with the *Ob–Kobra* complex.
- T-80U (Object 219AS): new turret with *Kontakt*-5 ERA, 1A42 *Irtysh* FCS, and *Refleks* GLATGM complex. Later production models have 1,250hp GTD-1250 gas turbines.

Neither Ukraine nor Russia are known to use the original T-80 at the time of writing, hence the following description will focus on the T-80B and T-80U. Post-Soviet modernisations of the T-80, such as the T-80UE-1 and T-80BVM, will be covered separately. Finally, the T-80UD, the T-80U's 'cousin' powered by a 6TD diesel engine instead of a gas turbine, serves as the basis for the Ukrainian BM *Oplot*, hence it will be covered separately in that section instead.

T-80BV seen during Victory Day parade rehearsals in Ekaterinburg, Russia, April 2020. (Schadribicus, LiveJournal)

T-80U of the 4th Guards Tank Division in 2011. As of 2023, it remains the only known Russian unit to operate the T-80U. (Vitaly Kuzmin)

Firepower

The 125mm 2A46-2, 2A46M-1, and 2A46M-4 main gun models used on the T-80 family are fully interchangeable with those on the T-64B.[146] They also share the same MZ-style autoloader as the T-64. The original 1976 T-80 had the same TPD-K1 sighting complex as contemporary T-72As and T-64As. However, the T-64B, which entered service around the same time, used the far superior *Ob* automated FCS and *Kobra* GLATGM complex. It was patently ridiculous for a tank that cost significantly more than the T-64B to have an inferior weapon system, so the T-80 was quickly modified into the T-80B to incorporate the *Ob–Kobra* complex as well. These were adopted virtually unchanged from the T-64B, and the reader is directed to refer to the T-64's 'Firepower' section for more information on them.

The T-80U uses a completely new integrated FCS (IFCS) originally developed for the Object 476, designated the 1A45 *Irtysh*.[147] The *Irtysh* IFCS uses the 1A42 gunner FCS with 1G46 gunner primary sight and laser rangefinder as well as the 1V528 digital ballistic computer. These improved upon the already impressive (for its

T-80U firing its main gun at the Golovenki training ground, Moscow, 2019. Note the distinctive exhaust shape of gas turbine-powered T-80s. (Mil.ru)

time) capabilities of the *Ob* FCS. The 1G46 sight also includes all the components of the 9K119 *Refleks* laser beam-riding GLATGM complex, and the more powerful liquid-cooled laser allows the 9M119 *Refleks* missile's full 5km range to be utilised, unlike on the T-72B. The *Irtysh* IFCS also features the TPN-4-49 *Buran*-PA image intensification night sight, which is claimed to have over double the range of the older *Kristall*-PA and TPN-1 night sights under the same conditions in passive mode (without illumination).[148]

The *Irtysh* FCS also includes the commander's PNK-4S sighting complex, centred around the TKN-4S *Agat*-S combined day/night primary sight. The *Agat*-S is fully stabilised in both the horizontal and vertical planes, a first for a Soviet tank.[149] This dramatically improved the T-80U's 'hunter-killer' capabilities to a level superior even to the contemporary Leopard 2 with the PERI-R17 panoramic commander sight, which lacked a night mode until the PERI-R17A2 was introduced in 1998 with thermal imaging.[150] The commander on a T-80U also has full authority over the FCS, allowing him to override the gunner and lay the gun himself if necessary. However, the PNK-4S does not have a ballistic computer or laser rangefinder, thus he can only rely on the *Agat*-S sight's stadia markings in this mode. The commander also has a screen that duplicates the feed from the *Agava*-2 gunner thermal sight on tanks equipped with it.

These features of the *Irtysh* IFCS meant that the T-80U was easily the most advanced Soviet tank in terms of fire control, with its only weakness being the lack of a thermal imaging sight. In the 1990s, a very small number of T-80Us received the *Agava*-2 thermal sight, especially those marketed abroad, but the vast majority continued using *Buran*-PA due to *Agava*'s high cost and low production numbers.[151] The rare T-80UK (Object 630A) command tank also has *Agava*-2. *Agava*-2 was already fairly outdated compared to contemporary Western thermal imaging sights when it entered service, since the Soviets failed to invest in the expensive technology required to build such things and had bet on cheaper passive night vision sights. However, it was still a significant improvement over the *Buran*-PA, with increased vision range and less influence from environmental lighting conditions. It also allowed for the IR searchlight to be done away with; T-80Us without *Agava*-2 or other thermal sights retain it or use the PL-1-01 IR pulse laser.

As usual, T-80 tanks of all models feature a coaxial 7.62mm PKT machine gun (1,250 rounds) and a 12.7mm *Utyos* heavy AAMG (300 rounds). However, for reasons known only to the chief weapons designer, the T-80B did not adopt the remote-controlled *Utyos* mount of the T-64A, and instead uses a manually operated mounting attached directly to the commander's cupola, which is also manually operated.[152] The combined weight of the AAMG and cupola is about 300kg, which the commander has to turn using his own strength, complicating his work of observing the battlefield using his primary TKN-3M sight or aiming the AAMG. The *Utyos*' weight and length also unbalances the cupola, making it even more difficult to rotate, especially when the tank is in motion or on a slope. The only advantage of this arrangement over the T-72's is that the *Utyos* can be aimed forward while the cupola is also facing forward; it still requires the commander to expose himself in order to operate the AAMG.

On most T-80Us, for some unfathomable reason (likely a cost-cutting measure), the AAMG mounting was changed to an even more primitive one consisting of three pedestal mounts surrounding the commander's cupola, with the *Utyos* swapped between them. The commander can lean out of his hatch to operate the *Utyos* but his field-of-fire while doing so is limited. It is more convenient for the commander to exit the hatch, which also allows him a greater

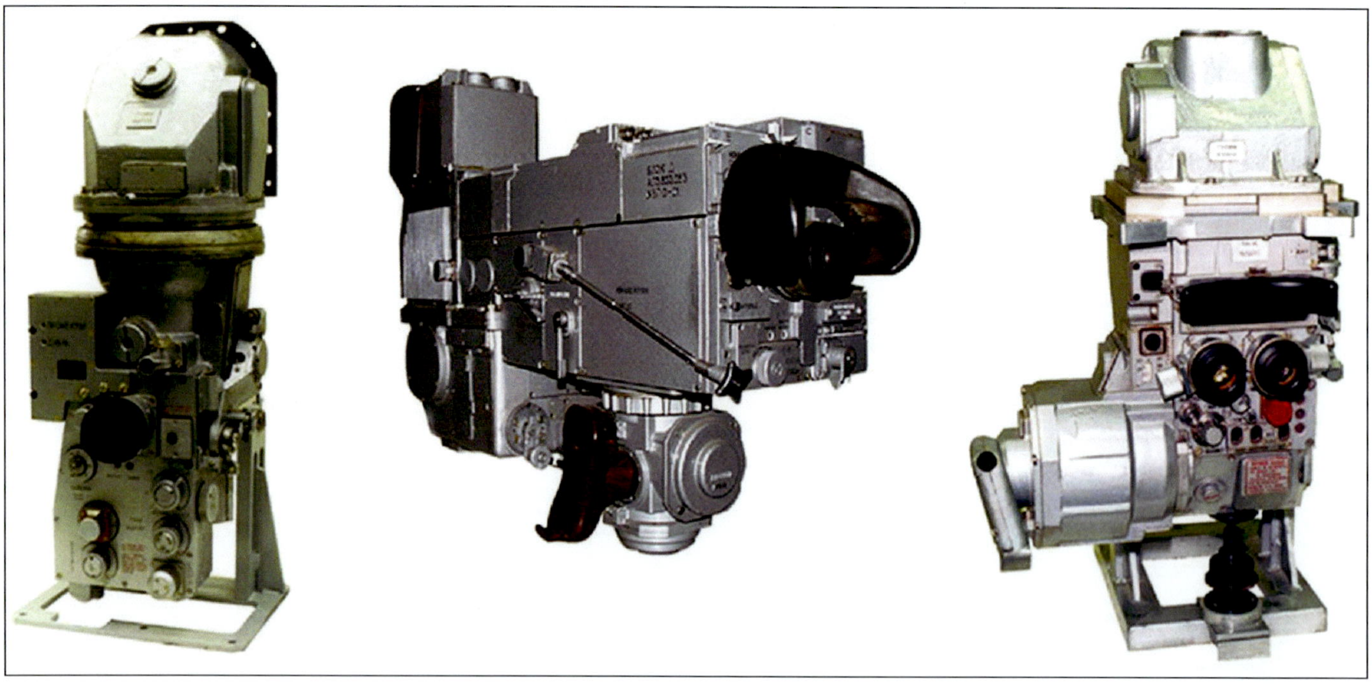

The three sights that form part of the *Irtysh* IFCS: from left to right, *Buran*-PA night sight, 1G46 gunner primary sight, and Agat-S commander's sight. (Kontenant)

field-of-fire, but leaves him completely exposed. To fire backwards, the *Utyos* has to be on the rear mount, and with a weight of 25kg, it is impractical to swap mounts during combat. The use of this system on the T-80U is even more perplexing considering that the related T-80UD used a remote-controlled AAMG mount.

The ammunition stowage arrangement on the T-80B is more or less identical to that of the T-64B (28 rounds in the MZ + eight extra rounds). It still uses the same 6ETs40-2S MZ as later T-64Bs. The T-80U has the newer 6ETs43 MZ, inherited from the *Kedr* project. The 6ETs43 can rotate in both directions instead of only clockwise and also has a slightly faster rotation speed, which decreases the average loading time (rated at 5.9 seconds). The T-80U's more spacious turret also allows for the extra stowage to be increased to 17 rounds, but requires putting 10 of these in the turret fighting compartment and greatly increases the risk of ammunition detonation if the turret is penetrated.

The awkwardly inconvenient AAMG mount of the T-80U in action. (Mil.ru)

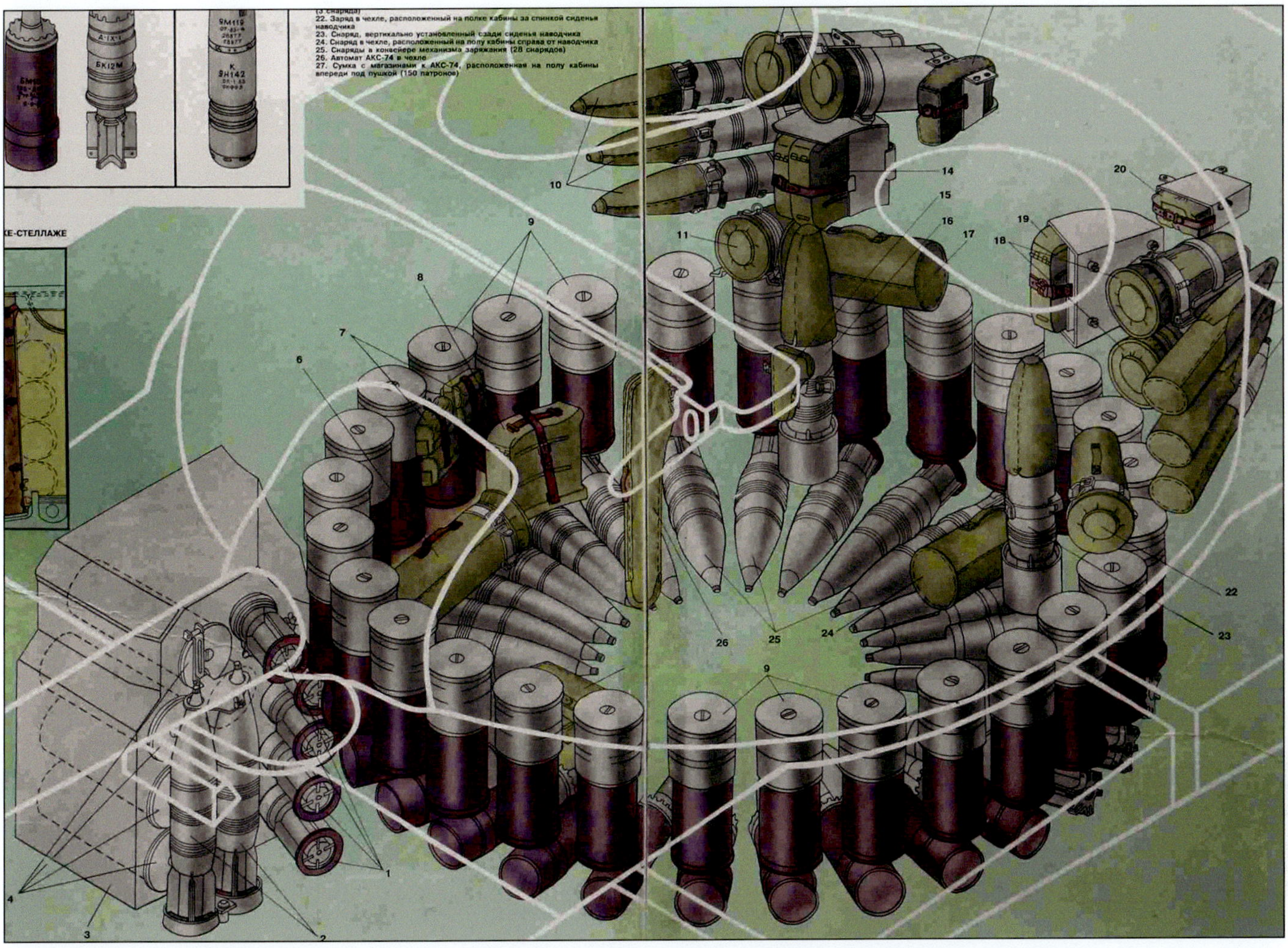

Ammo stowage in a T-80U. The turret rear stowage is a substantial hazard if the turret is penetrated. (Author's collection)

Protection

The original T-80 used the same protection layout as the original T-72 ('80-105-20' upper glacis and monolithic cast steel turret). The T-80B then adopted an armour configuration similar to that of the T-72A: 60mm RHA —100mm STB—45mm RHA sandwich for the upper glacis, and a slightly thicker *Kvartz*-type cast steel turret with sintered quartz filler. As with the T-64, this was reinforced with a 30mm applique plate on the upper glacis as a result of the *Otrazhenie* programme on existing tanks. The definitive T-80BV (Object 219RV) of 1985 uses a five-layer (RHA/STB/RHA/STB/RHA) upper glacis sandwich, with 50mm high-hardness RHA and 35mm STB layers. This provided somewhat better protection than the T-64BV's 60-35-30-35-45 five-layer glacis sandwich due to the thicker middle and backing plates.

The T-80U retained the same glacis as the T-80BV, but took a completely different approach to its turret composite armour protection. Inherited from the *Kedr* project's Object 476, the T-80U's cast turret has an outer thickness of 60–85mm, inner thickness of up to 190mm, and a 260mm cavity in between. This cavity is filled with a 'sandwich' comprising two layers (100mm and 60mm thick) of what is known as 'cellular filler' (*yacheistim napolnitelem*) armour with a 20mm HHA plate in between, and another 80mm HHA plate behind the sandwich.

'Cellular filler' is a type of non-explosive reactive armour (NERA) consisting of cast steel blocks with embedded 'cells' filled with polyurethane. A hit by the penetrating jet of a shaped charge causes a compression shock wave in the polyurethane, which in turn creates a secondary reflected compression shock wave when it reaches the polyurethane/steel boundary of the cell directed inwards towards the jet. The secondary wave collapses the polyurethane around the shaped charge jet, disrupting it and reducing its penetration characteristics. An armour plate is welded on top of the cavity, similar to the armour arrangement on the T-72B, and thus the 'cellular armour' can also be relatively easily replaced following battle damage by cutting off the roof plate and replacing the cellular filler blocks and patching any holes in the cast steel turret walls. Calculations and test results showed that for an equivalent amount of protection against shaped charges, this 'cellular armour' weighed 60 percent less than monolithic cast steel while having similar dimensions.[153]

The T-80BV also introduced the ubiquitous *Kontakt*-1 ERA package, consisting of 132 blocks (54 turret, 60 hull front, 18 hull side). The T-80BV's ERA package does not cover the side-skirts, unlike those of the T-72AV/B and T-64BV: during testing, it was found that the rubber-fabric side-skirts were not durable enough to take the added weight of the *Kontakt*-1 ERA blocks, and tended to flutter and buckle during movement. Thus, the side hull ERA protection is limited to a thin strake of single ERA blocks covering the fenders. It is unknown why the designers did not use the T-64BV's sturdier mounting frame arrangement for the side ERA blocks. The frontal hull and turret ERA coverage is also worse than on the T-64BV or T-72AV: the former is because the T-80B has two additional vision blocks for the driver. The reason for the worse turret ERA coverage (56 percent vs. 62 percent on the T-64BV and T-72AV) is unknown.[154]

A T-80B that slipped off a trailer, with the applique plate from the *Otrazhenie* programme on its upper glacis. Similar plates were applied to T-64s in the 1980s. (TheDeadDistrict, Twitter)

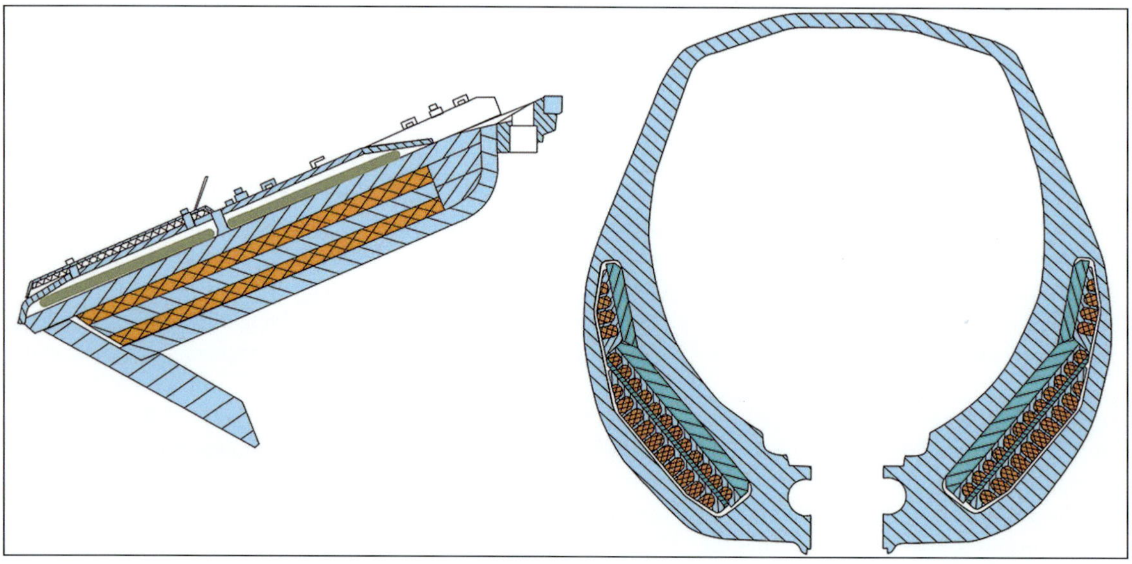

T-80U upper glacis and turret armour configurations. *Kontakt*-5 ERA is shown as well for the upper glacis. The orange parts in the turret are cells filled with polyurethane embedded in cast iron blocks, backed by HHA plates. (Andrei Tarasenko)

The earliest production T-80Us also used *Kontakt*-1. However, this was soon replaced by the superior *Kontakt*-5. The *Kontakt*-5 package on the T-80U has significantly better coverage than on the T-72B, about 60 percent of the frontal hull (15 containers) and turret surfaces (16 containers). The turret uses trapezoidal containers, each containing up to four 4S22 elements, instead of rectangular ones on the T-72B, thus leaving no gaps between the containers.[155] On the command T-80UK variant (and other T-80Us with *Agava*-2), the coverage is better because the *Luna*-2 searchlight was removed and the gap eliminated. Side hull coverage is provided by three large panels on each side with six (first panel) or nine elements (second and third panels). This arrangement provided significantly better side coverage than the three large square panels used on the T-72B, though it somewhat reduces the effectiveness against kinetic projectiles.[156] Swedish tests of a similar model to the T-80U turret composite armour package with *Kontakt*-5 showed that it was capable of withstanding the 120mm DM33 APFSDS fired by the German Rh 120 smoothbore gun used on the Leopard 2.[157] It was rated as similar in protection to the American M1A2 Abrams' turret, which the Swedes also tested.[158]

In addition to these features, the T-80B/BV and T-80U have the usual *Tucha* smoke grenade launchers, with a total of eight grenade launchers each. For unknown reasons, on the T-80U these are mounted directly on the *Kontakt*-5 turret ERA blocks instead of on the side of the turret like on T-80BVs with ERA, which means that they could be lost if the ERA is set off. On the T-80U, the driver's seat is also not attached to the bottom of the hull, but from the hull roof. There is also a metal pillar immediately behind the driver's seat. These features were intended to reduce the chance of injury to the driver from mine explosions.

Mobility

T-80UK putting its mobility on display in Omsk, 2009. Note the Shtora IR emitters on the turret front. (Vitaly Kuzmin)

The single most significant difference between the T-80 family and the T-64 and T-72 families is the T-80's use of a gas turbine engine as its main powerplant. Gas turbines (which include jet engines) operate on a completely different principle to diesel engines: they use the combustion of air drawn in by a compressor with fuel to drive a turbine, with the resulting mechanical energy used to both drive the compressor and, via a gearbox, propel the tank. T-80 gas turbines were developed and produced by the Klimov factory, with the T-80B and early production T-80Us using the 1,100hp GTD-1000TF, while post-1990 production T-80Us have the 1,250hp GTD-1250.[159]. A T-80B weighs 42 tonnes and a T-80U with GTD-1250 weighs 46 tonnes, giving them a power/weight ratio of about 27hp/t, significantly more than either the T-72 or T-64 can manage.

Gas turbine engines provide several major advantages over conventional diesel engines. The higher power output and torque of the GTD engines give the T-80 family excellent acceleration and manoeuvrability on decent terrain and the highest mobility of the Soviet tank families (at least on paper), often demonstrated in 'flying tank' displays by the T-80U during defence expos. In some situations, this can confer tactical advantages, such as the ability to move in and out of cover quickly.

Gas turbines are also much faster and easier to start up in very cold temperatures than diesel engines, since they do not require pre-warming: it takes three minutes to start up a T-80 in such temperatures, compared to 30 minutes for a T-72. This was one of the reasons why units such as the 200th Motor Rifle Brigade based in Murmansk near the Arctic Circle continued to use the T-80 even after Russia had mostly phased it out of service in favour of the T-72 family.[160] Gas turbines also do not require nearly as much lubricant oil as diesel engines.

However, these advantages come at a big price: very high fuel consumption. Gas turbines are at their most efficient at high power settings (i.e. speeds of 40–45km/h and above), where they can even exceed the fuel efficiency of diesel engines, but tanks rarely operate at such high speeds. They will spend a significant amount of time at lower speeds or idling, when the gas turbine will be consuming almost as much fuel as if the tank were running at full speed. During joint tests in 1976, it was found that to complete a 300km march, a T-80 required 60 percent more fuel than a T-64 and 80 percent more than a T-72. This much greater fuel consumption did not result in particularly huge speed gains in a march: the average marching speed of the T-80 unit in those tests was only 2 and 5km/h higher

The T-80U's GTD-1250 'monobloc' design combines the gas turbine engine, cooling, and air cleaning systems into one package that can be quickly changed in the field. (Author's collection)

than the T-72 and T-64 units, respectively.[161] The gas turbine engines were also vastly more expensive than a diesel engine and were the primary reason behind the T-80's higher price tag: according to Baryatinskiy, in 1980s prices, a V-46 cost ₽9,600, while a GTD-1000 cost over 10 times as much (₽104,000).[162]

To alleviate the fuel consumption problem, the T-80U has an auxiliary power unit (APU) consisting of the 30hp GTA-18A mini gas turbine and attached DC generator. This APU turbine could be switched on when idling or operating in stationary/defensive positions, allowing the primary gas turbine to be switched off while maintaining power to the tank's systems, reducing fuel consumption and engine wear. This is complemented by an automatic engine control system, first implemented on the T-80B, for better engine power management.

Gas turbine engines are not particularly fond of foreign object ingestion, so a cyclone air filter is provided. It is claimed that the filter will remove 97 percent of dust from the intake air, although this still allows dust and residue to build up on the turbine blades over time. To counteract this, the T-80 uses a unique 'vibro-cleaning' system consisting of miniature pneumatic vibrators tuned to the resonant frequency of the turbine blades, along with a high-pressure de-dusting system. The vibrations will shake off the residue from the blades, which are then blown away using high-pressure compressed air.[163]

The T-80s use BKP transmission units attached directly to the gas turbine. These differ from the T-64/T-72 BKPs in having only five forward gears (four in the T-80U) and one reverse gear, allowing for a top road speed of 70km/h and a reverse speed of 11km/h. The latter is significantly better than on any other Soviet tank, but still fairly low by modern Western MBT standards (many of which can do 30km/h or better in reverse). The GTD and BKPs are designed for easy and quick replacement: engine replacement can be done in 5.5 hours while each BKP took 4.5 hours to replace.[164] A similar operation on the T-72 would take 24 hours for the engine, 10.5 hours for each BKP, and another 17.7 hours for the gearbox connecting the engine to the BKPs.[165]

Because of the higher speed, starting with the T-80B the driver has three periscopes instead of a single one in order to give him a better view while 'buttoned up'. In general, a driver could not easily switch between the T-80 and the other Soviet MBTs without retraining, due to the very different controls and handling of the gas turbine engine. Despite the very high power/weight ratio of the T-80s, the outdated manual BKP lever controls make it driving more difficult and tiring. By the 1980s, Western tanks were using automatic transmissions with steering wheels or handles instead of the driver manually juggling the gears of two transmissions.

The Leningrad designers abandoned the T-64's small-diameter steel road wheels with internal shock absorbers and lightweight torsion bars in favour of more conventional rubber-rimmed road wheels and full-length offset torsion bars. The six aluminium alloy road wheels have more in common with the T-72, though they are of a different design. The higher dynamic loads also made it necessary to use five return rollers per side. The T-80s did, however, inherit the telescoping hydraulic shock absorbers of the T-64 (reinforced to handle the higher loads), plus they also have longer torsion keys than the T-72, with the associated benefits when it comes to ride smoothness.

The T-80's dual-pin tracks are based on the T-64's dual-pin tracks, but with some modifications: they do not have the distinctive holes in the track links and have inner rubber track pads in order to reduce wear on the rubber rims of the road wheels and vibrations when driving over rough terrain. However, it compromises the traction in mud, since the inner track surface is effectively flat due to the rubber pads and does not contribute to traction. They also increase power loss when moving at low speeds due to increased resistance. However, the traction is considered to be better than for the T-72's single-pin tracks.

The T-80 family has the most expensive running gear among the Soviet tanks. This is due to the large amount of non-ferrous alloys and materials (especially rubber and aluminium) used and the more complicated design (i.e. greater number of parts). In 1985 prices, the T-80 suspension (~₽35,000) cost over triple that of the T-64 (~₽11,000) and nearly 50 percent more than the T-72's (~₽25,000).[166] Combined with the price figures for the gas turbine engine, one begins to understand why the T-80 cost so much more than any other Soviet tank.

In order to satisfy the voracious appetite for fuel of the gas turbine engines, the T-80B and T-80U have greater fuel capacities than the T-64 or T-72. These can be supplemented by two 200 litre external fuel drums (three for T-80U). T-80s have an efficient pressurised central refuelling system, which cuts the refuelling time by about 40 percent compared to the T-64 or T-72.[167] The

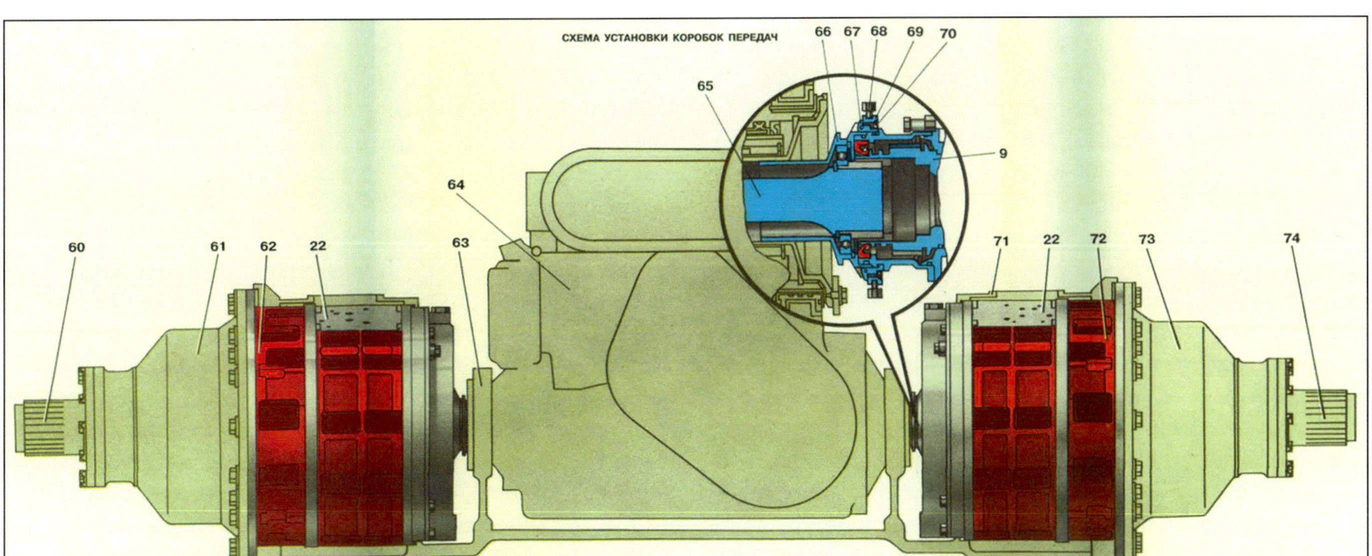

T-80U transmission system. The BKPs must be removed separately from the engine. (Author's collection)

GTD gas turbines primarily run on T-1 or TS-1-grade kerosene jet fuel, but they are also capable of accepting diesel fuel or jet fuel-diesel mixtures.

Results from the Swedish trials noted the T-80U's excellent suspension, acceleration, driver visibility, and obstacle-crossing capability. The Swedes were, however, critical of its antiquated steering system and low reverse speed. They also noted a tendency for the T-80U to lose traction due to mud building up in its tracks, which lack self-cleaning features. This limited its obstacle-crossing performance.[168]

Close-up of a T-80BV's road wheels and tracks. Note the inner rubber pads of the tracks. (Konstantin Popov, kpopov.ru)

Context

The T-80 family has a reputation in the West for being the 'premium' Soviet tanks, the ones reserved for such 'elite' units as those in East Germany or the 4th Guards Kantemirov Tank Division (4GTD) that usually participates in the Victory Day Red Square parades. Leaving aside the fact that this is a misunderstanding of how the Soviets allocated tanks, the T-80 family certainly had the price tag and performance on paper to justify such a reputation, especially comparing the T-80U to the contemporary T-72B.[169] Certainly, the T-80U was the most advanced MBT the Soviets had at the end of the Cold War, while the T-80B is, on paper, at least as capable as the T-64B and has superior mobility.

During the First Chechen War, at least 37 T-80B/BVs were lost during the Battle of Grozny fighting against the Chechen insurgents, mostly to ATGMs and handheld AT weapons.[170] These losses were mostly attributed to improper use of the tanks in urban fighting by the inexperienced and poorly trained crews. This was not helped by the fact that many of these tanks did not have the explosive inserts in their *Kontakt*-1 ERA blocks due to incompetence in the supply chain (tanks usually did not have the inserts fitted during training or storage, and they were sent into battle without them).[171]

Following the Chechen War, the VSRF chose the more economical T-72/T-90 family instead. After all, if the more expensive T-80's combat performance was not significantly better than the T-72's, what was the point? T-80 production at the Omsktransmash factory ended in 2001.[172] This, in combination with the failure of the T-80U to secure significant export orders, resulted in Omsktransmash going bankrupt and eventually getting absorbed by UVZ, sealing UVZ's dominance over the Russian tank industry. Today, Omsktransmash engages only in refurbishment and modernisation of the existing T-80 fleet. As of September 2021, the VSRF had 443 T-80s of all models in service, including the modernised T-80UE-1 and T-80BVM models, which will be covered separately. The aforementioned 4GTD is the only known unit in the VSRF that uses T-80Us.

Ukraine inherited 248 T-80s after the fall of the USSR, of which 188 were T-80s or T-80B/BVs and the remainder T-80UDs.[173] However, it did not use the former prior to the start of the Russo–Ukrainian War in 2014, having chosen to focus exclusively on the domestically produced T-64 and looking to the T-80UD for the future. However, the need to replace losses has led to the ZSU restoring T-80BVs into service. These primarily equipped the tank companies of the air assault and marine brigades, where the T-80's higher speed is better appreciated by these rapid reaction units. Prior to the 2022 invasion, each brigade had a company of 10 T-80BVs. In 2018, the ZSU initiated a T-80BV upgrade programme (see Part 2). Following the 2022 invasion, especially after the debacle suffered by the 4GTD in the Kyiv–Chernihiv–Sumy axis, Ukraine has also

In March 2022, five 4GTD T-80Us became stuck in the mud while invading Chernihiv oblast and were abandoned by their crews. They were captured by the ZSU and pressed into service. (ZSU)

captured large numbers of T-80BVs and T-80Us and pressed these into service, including at least one very rare T-80UK command tank.

One thing that still is an issue with the T-80s is their high fuel consumption. In a 2018 interview with News.ru, Khlopotov noted that the actual fuel consumption rate of T-80s is two to three times more than what is written in the documented specifications.[174] This proved less of an issue in the Chechen War, where the Chechens were less able to interdict Russian logistics, although it was noted. However, during the initial stages of the 2022 invasion, the better-equipped ZSU were able to punish the poorly protected Russian supply lines. This denied T-80 units like 4GTD their invaluable fuel supplies, eventually forcing the Russians to abandon them en masse. This was further exacerbated by the T-80's relatively poor performance on muddy terrain.

Ukrainian T-80BVs appear to have met with more success. Many, if not all, of them have been modernised, as will be discussed later. The Ukrainian 25th Airborne and 80th Air Assault Brigades' and their T-80BVs were among the units that spearheaded the Kharkiv counteroffensive of September 2022, using the firepower and mobility of their tanks to punch through the weakened Russian forces in the region and instigating a rout of the demoralised soldiers, forcing the Russians to withdraw completely from Kharkiv *oblast*.[175] The offensive also resulted in the capture of hundreds of Russian vehicles, including more T-80s from the 1st Guards Tank Army (1GTA), which was still in the process of rebuilding after their defeat near Kyiv.[176]

It is unknown if either Russia or Ukraine will retain their T-80s after the war. Ukraine does not produce the T-80, but has found itself operating a fairly large fleet of T-80 tanks captured from the Russians. Whether it will be able or wants to sustain this large fleet over the long-term is uncertain. Russian T-80 losses have been staggering: as of January 2023, the VSRF has been visually confirmed to have lost at least 202 T-80BVs and 89 T-80Us. This represents nearly 2/3rds of the pre-invasion active T-80 fleet.[177] Given the fact that new T-80s are no longer being produced, these can only be replaced by older units reactivated from storage or with other types such as the T-72.

Captured T-80U in Ukrainian service with the 30th Mechanised Brigade. Note that this T-80U has a PL-1 pulse beamer replacing the *Luna* searchlight. (ZSU)

Ukrainian T-64BV of the 92nd Mechanised Brigade, 2015. This was one of the more well-trained and experienced Ukrainian military units in 2014, and remains one of the best today. (David Bocquelet)

LNR T-64BV No. 09 '*Za Donbass*' ('For Donbass'), 2014. For unknown reasons, it has the marking 'T-84' on its side. The flag on the turret is that of 'Novorossiya'. (David Bocquelet)

Russian T-72A of the 239th Guards Tank Regiment, 90th Guards Tank Division. It was captured in Khvylivka, Nizhyn on 2 March 2022 after it was abandoned. (David Bocquelet)

Russian T-72B *'Karavan'*, Zaporizhzhia oblast, January 2023. This is an early T-72B with *Kontakt*-1 ERA. (David Bocquelet)

DNR T-72B No. 374 *'Somali'*, 2014. It has the N2200 railway marking used by Russian railways to mark oversized cargo, indicating it was delivered from Russia. (David Bocquelet)

Russian T-72B of the 239th Guards Tank Regiment, 90th Guards Tank Division. It was knocked out in the Brovary region on 9 April 2022 and captured by Ukrainian forces. (David Bocquelet)

Russian T-80BV 'Sibir' ('Siberia') of ChVK *Vagner*, seen in Rostov-on-Don during the *Vagner* rebellion on 23 June 2023. (David Bocquelet)

Russian T-80U No. 480 of the 4th Guards Tank Division. Abandoned in Sumy, it was captured by Ukrainian forces on 11 March 2022 and later put on display in Kyiv alongside other captured or destroyed Russian hardware. (David Bocquelet)

Russian T-90A No. 516 of the 20th Motor Rifle Division, abandoned and captured by Ukrainian forces at Posad-Pokrovske, Kherson on 27 February 2022. The tank was missing its side ERA panels when it was recovered. (David Bocquelet)

Russian T-72B3 in Victory Day Parade colours, Ekaterinburg, 2021. This tank was abandoned in Nizhyn on 7 April 2022, captured by Ukrainian forces, and later destroyed, still painted in these colours. (David Bocquelet)

Russian T-72B3M No. 717 of the 1st Tank Regiment, 2nd 'Taman' Guards Motor Rifle Division. It was abandoned and captured by Ukrainian forces at Perevolochna, Pryluky on 27 February 2022. (David Bocquelet)

Russian 'Mobilisation' T-72B3 built after February 2022 with more extensive ERA coverage, unknown unit. (David Bocquelet)

Russian T-80BVM No. 739 of the 200th Motor Rifle Brigade, as seen after being abandoned, captured by Ukrainian forces on 2 March 2022. (David Bocquelet)

Captured T-80BVM No. 739 in Ukrainian service with the 93rd 'Khlodnyi Yar' Mechanised Brigade as 'Zayka' ('Bunny'). The tank served with the brigade until it became stuck in mud during the Battle of Bakhmut in April 2023 and was abandoned. It was destroyed to prevent recapture. (David Bocquelet)

Russian T-90M, unknown unit, as seen on a tank transporter in Melitopol, October 2022. These are the most advanced tanks fielded by Russian forces. (David Bocquelet)

2
RUSSIAN POST-SOVIET TANKS

T-90M *Proryv* (left), T-72B3 (middle), and T-80BVM (right) during the 2020 Victory Day Parade in Red Square, Moscow. These were the most advanced tanks fielded by the VSRF at the beginning of the 2022 invasion. (Nikolai Novichkov)

Following the end of the Cold War and the collapse of the Soviet Union, the precarious state of the Russian economy meant that it could no longer support the vast tank fleet it inherited from the Soviet Union. This had a few implications:

- Dramatic reductions in the number of active Russian tanks, with many older types like the T-62 and T-55 put into storage or scrapped.
- Phasing out of the T-64 and T-80UD from Russian service by 2010, due to the fact that they were built in the newly independent Ukraine and parts supply could not be guaranteed.
- Standardising on the T-72 family as the primary MBTs of the new Russian army.
- Increased dependence on exports to fund Russian tank development. In particular, India's 1998 decision to buy and license-build the T-90S in large numbers can probably be credited with saving the Russian tank industry and UVZ's current preeminent position as the leading Russian tank manufacturer.

Russian post-Cold War tank development efforts have mostly been directed towards modernising their Soviet legacy T-72 and T-80 tanks. These have come in the form of the T-90A, T-72B3, T-80BVM, and T-90M tanks. These decisions were mostly driven by the perceived need to keep up with the improved MBTs being fielded by NATO, such as the German Leopard 2A6, French Leclerc, and American M1A2 SEP, which severely outclassed the T-72 and T-80 in almost all aspects, while their economic limitations and development problems have so far prevented Russia from fielding the completely new *Armata* platform.

A common theme that one will see for the Russian modernisations is that they tend to focus particularly on improving the firepower of their tanks. A 1987 Soviet paper on evaluating tank technical qualities concluded that the most mass-efficient way to improve a tank is to increase its firepower via things like improved ammunition or more advanced night sights.[1] Soviet and Russian doctrine places a great emphasis on keeping the mass of their MBTs as low as possible, thus this theme is not surprising. As noted in the introduction, the Soviets had a fondness for applying complex mathematical models to military matters (operations research), which the Russians have inherited: a 2011 paper on evaluating tank effectiveness gave the number of input variables and constants for the mathematical models used at 1,586, with 1,970 outputs.[2] These models place a lot of emphasis on improving 'hard' factors like in the firepower/mobility/protection trifecta, since they are easier to quantify. However, they seem to underrate 'soft' factors: only the T-90A and T-90M received 'luxuries' like a satellite navigation system (SNS), or a battlefield management system (BMS) and commander's independent thermal viewer (CITV) in the latter, all of which would be considered indispensable in a Western MBT today. Where economies have to be made, such as on the T-72B3 or T-80BVM, these features are usually dropped.

In general, the Russian tank industry does not build many completely new hulls from scratch today: only UVZ is presently capable of and has the resources to actually build new tanks. All the other Russian 'tank factories' are what are known as 'AFV repair factories' (*bronetankoviy remontniy zavod*, BTRZ). These are responsible for repairs and upgrades but do not have the facilities to, say, assemble an entirely new hull from scratch. The T-72B3 and T-80BVM are made from existing T-72B and T-80BV tanks, and even some of the T-90As and T-90Ms are rebuilds of existing tanks.

Annual Russian tank production prior to February 2022 (including upgrades and refurbishments) was about 200 tanks. In September 2021, out of the 2,609 Russian tanks in service at the time, 1,340 (51 percent) were tanks built or upgraded after 2000. Another 12 battalions were in the process of formation (making for an additional 12 x 31 = 372 tanks): it is not known whether these had finished forming by February 2022, though it is unlikely given the relatively low annual production rate.[3]

It should be noted that there is significantly less publicly available information about post-Cold War Russian MBTs, since many of them entered service relatively recently. Hence, the sections here will be shorter than those in the 'Soviet Legacy Tanks' chapter. Much of the information is sourced from export brochures, manufacturers' claims at defence expos, news publications, and certain knowledgeable defence analysts connected to the Russian tank industry such as Khlopotov. The former should be taken with a grain of salt, especially their propensity for hyperbole like '*ne imeyushchiy analogov*' ('without analogues' i.e. 'unparalleled').

As a final note, this book will not discuss the T-14 (Object 148), the MBT variant of the *Armata* universal combat platform. It has not reached production or service status and, despite spurious claims, there is no evidence that the T-14 has seen combat or been deployed to Ukraine at the time of writing. There is also much less concrete information about the T-14 and its systems.

2.1: T-90A: Marketing Exercise?

T-90A rehearsing for the Battle of Stalingrad anniversary parade in Volgograd, January 2023. (RIAC34.ru)

The T-90 (Object 188) started its life as an improvement programme for the T-72B dating back to the late 1980s, incorporating some of the advanced features found on the T-80U and fixing some weaknesses of the T-72. Indeed, according to Suvorov and Khlopotov, the tank was originally designated T-72BM during development and later 'advanced T-72B' (*T-72B usovershentsvovanniy*). At some point the name was changed to T-90 before the tank entered service in 1992. It is often claimed that Russian President Boris Yeltsin was responsible for the name change, but Khlopotov disputes this.[4]

It is also often speculated that the reason behind this renaming was to distance the T-90 from the poor performance of the T-72 in Iraqi service during the previous year's Operation Desert Storm, where they were savaged by the American M1A1 Abrams and British Challenger tanks of the Coalition forces. Of course, the Iraqis were using export T-72M1s firing inferior ammunition, and were also worn out from the heavy fighting of the Iran–Iraq War, but this did not help the T-72's reputation. No documentary evidence proves Desert Storm played a role in the renaming.

In 1996, Russia would standardise on the T-90 as its sole MBT, with the T-80U slowly phased out of production.[5] Yeltsin was coincidentally the Communist Party's First Secretary of the Sverdlovsk *oblast* from 1979–1985, where the city of Nizhny Tagil and UVZ are located; whether his possible connections to UVZ had anything to do with this decision is an open question. This was all academic anyway in the 1990s, as Russia could not afford to order enough T-90s to economically sustain UVZ. However, a large export order and license production agreement with India for the T-90S Bhishma brought much needed funding that allowed UVZ to continue development work. It would not be an exaggeration to say that the T-90 saved the Russian tank industry from total collapse this way.

Officially, the VSRF no longer uses the original T-90s, relegating them to storage or training units; it uses the T-90A (Object 188A), introduced in 2004 with an angular welded turret incorporating elements from the Indian export T-90S *Bhishma* variant.[6] This will thus be the model covered in this book. The most advanced T-90A model is the T-90A1 (Object 188A1) with BMS integration and *Essa* thermal sight.[6] There is also the T-90AK command tank variant, of which very little is known. It is thought to contain improved communications and navigation equipment, as expected for command tanks. The T-90M, which entered production in 2019, is substantially different from the T-90A, hence it will be covered separately.

T-90S '*Zubr*' formerly in service with ChVK *Vagner* 'mercenaries' reappropriated by the Russian military following the end of the *Vagner* rebellion in July 2023. Note the lack of *Shtora* IR emitters. It is not presently known if the Russians are using export demonstrator/surplus tanks or requisitioning T-90Ss sent back by India to Russia for upgrading. (Mil.ru)

Firepower

The biggest improvements that the T-90s boast over the T-72B are in firepower. The T-90A uses the improved 125mm 2A46M-5 smoothbore main gun. which has minor improvements to increase accuracy. The modified AZ-185-3S autoloader is compatible with longer projectiles such as the modern 3BM59 *Svinets*-1 and 3BM60 *Svinets*-2 long-rod APFSDS.[8] This feat was accomplished by pulling the cassette back as it is lifted in order to give it enough clearance to get past the gun breech.[9] Modifying the AZ for this is non-trivial: it requires modifications to the AZ receiving tray, cassette lifting mechanism, and carousel.[10] All T-90As are also capable of firing the 9M119 *Refleks* family of GLATGMs.

The T-90A also uses the 1A45T *Irtysh* FCS, modified from the original *Irtysh* FCS used on the T-80U. It shares most of the features and components, but a new *Buran*-M image intensifier night sight with increased range was installed instead. From 2008 onwards, T-90As began receiving the Belarusian Peleng *Essa* thermal sight,

T-90A fires its main gun. The commander cupola and remote Utyos AAMG mounting are visible to the right. (Dmitriy Meshcheryakov, Drive2.ru)

based around the French Catherine-FC thermal imaging camera. First used on the export T-90S, *Essa* is a significant improvement over both the *Buran*-M and the earlier *Agava*-2 thermal sight used on the T-80U and T-90, boasting independent two-plane stabilisation and integration with the 1V528-1 ballistic computer.[11] The commander's sight has been also replaced with the *Agat*-M, featuring an improved image intensifier with greater range.

The T-90A also has the *Aynet* programmable munitions complex.[12] First developed for the T-80UK and entering service in 1988, *Aynet* can use data from the rangefinder and ballistic computer to automatically set the programmable fuses of the 3OF54 HE-Frag and 3Sh7 and 3Sh8 flechette rounds with the UVI-11 fuse-setter to allow air-bursts, enhancing their lethality against infantry or soft-skinned vehicles.[13] In previous Soviet and Russian tanks, the loading process has to be interrupted in order to manually set the time fuses of air-burst munitions. UKBTM claims that these programmable munitions are five to seven times more effective than point-detonating (impact) HE-Frag shells against exposed infantry.[14]

Another significant departure of the T-90A from both the T-72B and T-80U was the use of a remote AAMG mount. It is taken from the Kharkov-built T-80UD. The commander can aim the AAMG using the PZU-7 sight and fire it without exposing himself. The mount is fully stabilised as well and can be slaved to the *Agat*-M commander sight. This gives it significantly more utility than the questionable manually operated AAMG mounts of the T-72B or T-80U, especially in urban environments. Either *Utyos* or its modern replacement, the 12.7mm *Kord*, can be used as the AAMG.

Protection

Diagram published in a UKBTM brochures with a T-90S turret, suggesting that the cavity is filled with the same 'reflecting plates' used on the T-72B. (Alexey Khlopotov)

Whereas the original T-90 inherited the same turret from the T-72B, the T-90A adopted a new welded turret with rolled plates originally developed for the Indian T-90S. In general, cast armour has worse ballistic resistance than a rolled armour plate of an equivalent mass, and it has been abandoned on pretty much every modern MBT. The T-90A's turret front consists of 65mm front and 150mm rear medium hardness plates with a large cavity in between.[15]

The turret's protection is further enhanced by the *Kontakt*-5 ERA package. This consists of eight ERA blocks on the turret front and another 21 smaller blocks on the turret roof to help protect against top-attack munitions. However, the turret front coverage is compromised by the fitting of the IR projectors associated with the TShU-1-7 *Shtora* complex. As a result, less than 50 percent of the turret is covered against frontal attacks.[16] On the Indian T-90S, extra turret ERA coverage was preferred, and the IR projectors were removed. The hull armour package is more or less identical to that of the late-1980s T-72B with *Kontakt*-5.

The *Shtora* ('Curtain') electro-optical countermeasures complex is a 'soft-kill' active protection system (APS) designed to protect the T-90A from laser-guided anti-tank missiles and projectiles. First introduced on the T-80UK, *Shtora* is a suite of laser detectors covering the front and sides of the turret and two distinctive IR projectors. The laser detectors can automatically aim the turret at a detected emitter. This allows the tank to quickly react against a potential threat to return fire or deploy smoke grenades to block the laser source, as well as pointing the strongest armour of the turret against a potential

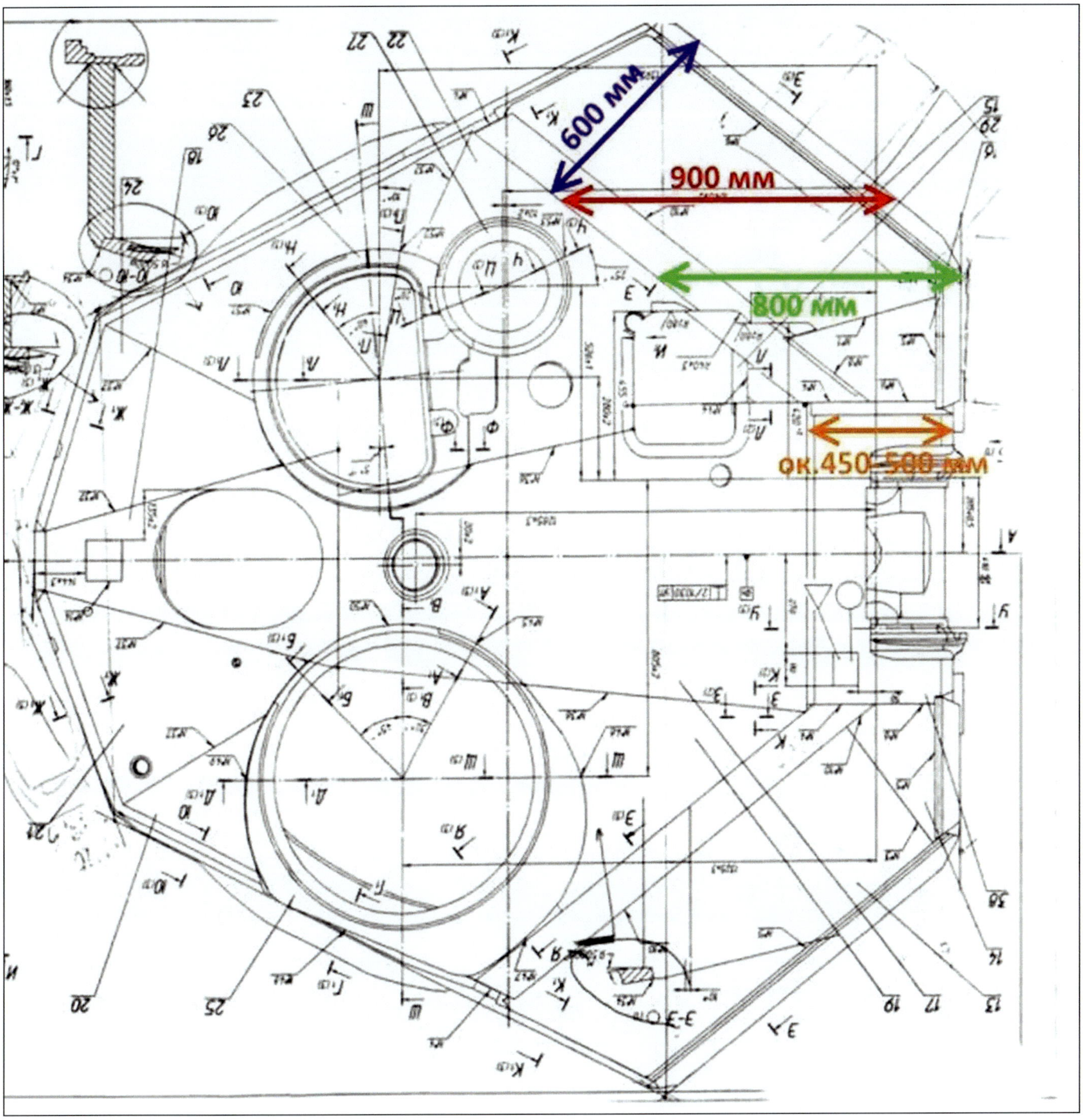

Blueprint for the T-90S turret with thickness measurements. The T-90A's turret is similar, if not identical. (Otdetie v Broni)

incoming projectile. The IR projectors can 'blind' the optical trackers of certain SACLOS ATGMs, which must 'see' the IR flare at the rear of the missile in order to send the correct guidance commands. They must be turned on manually and pointed in the direction of an incoming missile, which requires the commander to have spotted the missile launch or pre-emptively aimed the turret in a potential missile launch's direction. There are 12 smoke grenade launchers integrated into the *Shtora* complex, which can automatically launch the grenades in the direction of a laser emitter.[17]

Shtora has no effect on unguided projectiles and is also useless against the American FGM-148 Javelin top-attack fire-and-forget ATGM supplied in large numbers to Ukraine, a heat-seeking missile. The TOW-2, a SACLOS missile, is also upgraded with an encoded IR flare and a xenon beacon, which negate the blinding effect of the *Shtora*'s IR projectors. During the Syrian Civil War, the TOW-2A successfully knocked out several T-90As in spite of their *Shtora* systems.[18]

T-90A with *Shtora* IR emitters activated. Note the gaps in the *Kontakt*-5 ERA coverage created by the emitters. (Sputnik)

Mobility

T-90A on the move. The *Shtora* IR emitters and laser warning receivers above the main gun are readily visible, as is the *Essa* gunner thermal sight. (Mil.ru)

In terms of mobility, the T-90A is mostly identical to the T-72B. The original T-90 kept the 840hp V-84 engine, but this was found to be underpowered because the T-90's weight had increased to 46.5 tonnes, dropping the power/weight ratio to 18hp/t. The T-90A uses the boosted V-92S2 engine featuring a turbocharger to increase the power output to 1,000hp. This brought the power/weight ratio up to a respectable 21.5hp/t. The suspension and transmission components of the T-90A remain virtually unchanged from the T-72B, other than some strengthening to withstand the increased weight of the tank.

Because of the poor durability and performance issues of the original single-pin tracks of the T-72, a new dual-pin 'live' track was developed by UKBTM for the T-90. It is based on the T-80's tracks, but lacks the inner rubber pads. This eliminates power loss due to the higher rolling resistance on the inner rubber track pads while at the same time reducing high power-loss experienced on the T-72 when running at high speeds due to the more flexible dual-pin design, effectively combining the better attributes of both track designs. The trade-off is the increased complexity of the track design when it comes to maintenance and repair. This track can also be used on late production T-72Bs.[19]

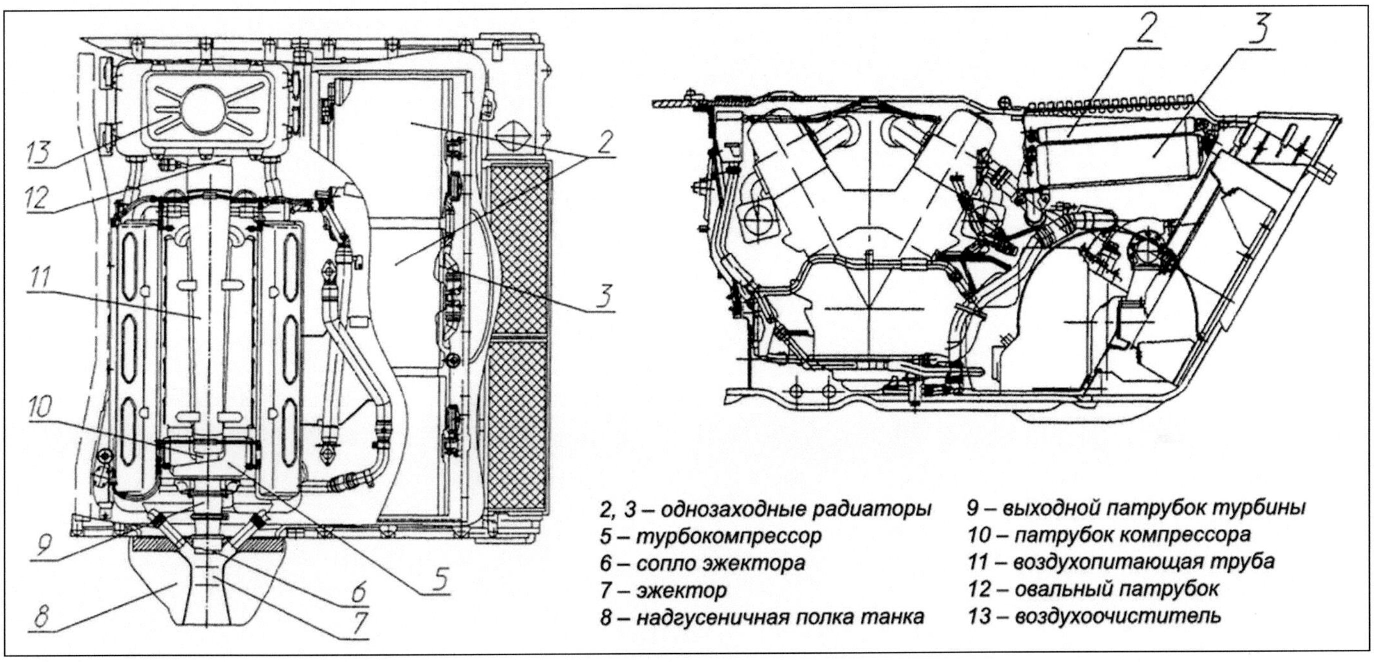

T-90A engine compartment with the V-92S2 1,000hp V-12 engine. The T-72 ancestry is obvious here. (Andrei Tarasenko)

Context

As Russia's first post-Cold War MBT, the T-90A basically attempts to rectify the worst flaws of the original T-72 tanks, especially by bringing the FCS up to the level of the T-80U and incorporating a greater degree of automation. The *Essa* thermal sight gives it a massive edge over previous Soviet and Russian tanks in terms of night-fighting capability. It was even the first Russian tank to incorporate network-centric warfare features with the T-90A1.

That said, the T-90A still inherits much from the T-72, for better or worse. The hull armour is virtually unchanged from the late-1980s T-72B with *Kontakt*-5. The T-90A also still uses the same suspension and BKP transmission: it still has the T-72's atrocious reverse speed and obsolete manual dual tiller lever steering system. While the V-92S2 engine upgrade improved the tactical mobility, the T-90A was not nearly on par with the T-80U in that respect. It also still suffers the same problems with mud, since this drawback is inherent in the T-72's suspension design.

In September 2021, the VSRF had approximately 200 T-90As in active service, making them the smallest tank contingent in the VSRF, excluding the new T-90M. They primarily served in the independent tank battalions attached to certain motor rifle regiments or brigades.[20] Production of the T-90A ended in 2010 in anticipation of the introduction of the T-14 *Armata*, with the T-72B3 upgrade programme intended as a stopgap. However, 13 years later, the T-14 is still nowhere close to being operational, and this led to the T-90M being developed and adopted for service, with some T-90As being rebuilt into T-90Ms as well.

In 2016, the open-source intelligence organisation Bellingcat published evidence showing that T-90As operated by Russian personnel participated in the 2014 Battle of Ilovaisk and in combat near Luhansk.[21] Given the secrecy surrounding Russia's involvement in the pre-2022 stages of the Russo–Ukrainian War, it is not possible to have a clear picture of how much the T-90A may have contributed to the defeat inflicted on the Ukrainians at Ilovaisk. However, at that time, the ZSU was equipped almost exclusively with Soviet legacy tanks and AT weapons, which would have been at a significant disadvantage against the T-90A.

At a 2018 talk held by the Russian Centre for Analysis of Strategies and Technologies (CAST), Anton Lavrov noted that the T-90As in Syria used by pro-Assad forces were 'not handled particularly skillfully'.[22] The same must also be said for Russian T-90As during the 2022 Russian invasion: whereas Assadist T-90As played a decisive role in securing victory in the 2016 Battle of Aleppo, Russian T-90As have not met with a similar level of success in 2022.[23] To give one example, the Russian 27th Guards Motor Rifle Brigade operated 20 T-90As in September 2021. According to captured documents, the brigade had lost almost half of them (nine) by 15 March 2022 while fighting in Sumy as part of the 1st Guards Tank Army before the VSRF was forced to abandon its offensive against Kyiv.[24]

Ukraine has captured at least 13 T-90As: one was sent to the Aberdeen Proving Ground in the US for testing in April 2023.[25] A fair number were 'appropriated' from 27 Guards Motor Rifle Brigade following the Russian debacles in Sumy and during the Kharkiv counteroffensive: the commander of 92nd 'Ivan Sirko' Mechanised Brigade (92 Mech.), Colonel Pavlo Fedosenko personally drove off with one captured during the latter.[26] Ukrainian tankers like SR have been quite complimentary about the T-90A and are quite respectful of its capabilities. As always, it is the men behind the machines that are most important of all.

T-90As of the Russian 136th Motor Rifle Brigade invading Luhansk *oblast*, Ukraine in 2014. The crews applied green paint to hide their markings, but were kind enough to take pictures of Ukrainian road signs and post them on social media. (RU social media)

Captured T-90A 'Maestro'. Like all members of the T-72 family, the exhaust port is on the tank's left side. (SR)

2.2: T-72B3: Old Tank, New Tricks

T-72B3 of the Southern Military District during exercises in Abkhazia, March 2020. The *Sosna*-U multispectral gunner sight has its armoured shutter open. One of the side *Kontakt*-5 panels is not fitted. (Mil.ru)

Faced with the obsolescence of its large T-72 fleet, but unable to afford procuring the T-90 in the numbers needed to replace the T-72, Russia opted to modernise the T-72s it had. The first T-72 upgrade programme was the T-72BA (Object 184A/A1) between 1998 and 2005. This was essentially a minor upgrade programme dedicated to bringing older T-72Bs up to the T-90 standard with *Kontakt*-5 ERA, dual-pin tracks, a DVE-BS wind sensor, and other improvements. Subsequently, they would receive upgrades to the AZ autoloader and the 1,000hp V-92S2 engine.[27]

However, this upgrade did not do much to improve the hopelessly outdated 1A40 FCS, which still lacked automatic lead and elevation and thermal sights. A much more comprehensive modernisation programme was proposed, called '*Rogatka*' ('Slingshot'). The *Rogatka* (also known as T-72B2 or Object 184M) had completely overhauled protection using the new *Relikt* ERA and the laser detectors of the *Shtora* complex, a modified autoloader to take modern ammunition like the T-90A, the *Sosna*-U ('Pine') integrated gunner thermal sight and FCS, the V-92S2 engine, and improved R-168 radio and SNS with BMS integration.[28]

Alas, Russia could not afford to modernise so many T-72s to such a high standard either. So, for the next proposed T-72 upgrade programme, some features were cut, such as the V-92S2 engine, the SNS and BMS, the laser detectors, and most of the *Relikt* ERA package. It was this 'stripped-down' package that was accepted by the VSRF as the T-72B3 in 2011.[29] The manual refers to it as '*Izdelie 184 (184-1) s PNM "Sosna-U"*' ('Product 184 (184-1) with *Sosna*-U multi-channel gunner sight'), indicating the primacy of the Sosna-U thermal imager and that it is an upgrade of existing T-72B/B1s.

It is important to note that there is not one type of 'T-72B3'; there are in fact at least three T-72B3s based on the years they were produced:

- 2011–2015: original variant with *Sosna*-U, modified autoloader, improved radio of *Rogatka*.
- 2016–2021: improved 1,130hp V-92S2F engine, automatic transmission, *Relikt* side armour package.
- 2022 onwards: incorporates 'combat experience' from the war mostly by slathering as much ERA as possible on every part of the tank.[30]

To distinguish between the original T-72B3 and the 2016 one with the upgraded engine, the latter will be referred to as 'T-72B3M' in this book.[31] The 2022 version shall simply be referred to as the 'mobilisation T-72B3'. There is not much information about this variant, so the description in this chapter will focus on the T-72B3 and T-72B3M.

T-72B3 of the Western Military District fires its gun, 2017. (Mil.ru)

Firepower

All T-72B3s use the 125mm 2A46M-5 main gun, as on the T-90A. There are references to T-72B3s using the 2A46M-5-01, but it is unknown how this gun differs from the 2A46M-5, if at all.[32] The T-72B3 also incorporates the same modifications to the autoloader that allow T-90As to fire longer projectiles, although the T-72B3's autoloader is distinct from the T-90A's AZ-185-S3. Ammunition stowage remains virtually unchanged at 22 rounds in the AZ and another spare 22 scattered around the driver and fighting compartments.

The T-72B3 and T-72B3M use the 1A40-4 FCS. This is built around the *Sosna*-U thermal sight with independent two-plane stabilisation. Like the T-90A's *Essa*, it was developed by the Belarusian Peleng company and is based on the French Catherine-FC thermal camera. Russia has acquired the licence to build both the *Sosna*-U and Catherine-FC, but early *Sosna*-Us used cameras imported from France with the Thales control panel. *Sosna*-U is connected with an automatic target-tracking system using sophisticated digital image processing: all the gunner has to do is put the crosshairs on a potential target and press a button, the system will do the rest. It is also compatible with the *Refleks* GLATGM, with guidance accomplished using the built-in laser rangefinder.

The original TPD-K1 rangefinder-sight is retained as a backup in the primary gunner sight position, while the *Sosna*-U occupies the former auxiliary night sight's space, which makes it somewhat inconvenient to use since the gunner has to crane his neck to the left to use the scope. A display screen is therefore also provided for the gunner, with the feed also duplicated for the commander on his own screen. The commander can lay and fire the gun by himself if necessary. Otherwise, the commander's equipment is virtually unchanged from that of a 1980s T-72B with the manually operated cupola, AAMG, and unstabilised *Kristall*-PA sight. Thus, his situational awareness in the T-72B3 is no better than in older

This abandoned T-72B3M with the inscription 'Taman Power' (suggesting it is from the 2nd 'Taman' Guards Motor Rifle Division) was penetrated by an APFSDS round fired by a Ukrainian tank in the side of the turret in May 2022. The gunner suffered a fatal head wound and died instantaneously. The Thales control panel and (broken) viewscreen for the *Sosna*-U can be seen to the right. The former shows that this *Sosna*-U has an imported French thermal camera. (Rhino1bamabm, Reddit)

tanks unless he takes over the gunner's controls. The T-72B3 can use the 12.7mm *Kord* as its AAMG instead of the old *Utyos*.

A news report by Izvestiya in January 2023 showed a T-72B3-like upgrade with a different thermal sight, the 1PN-96MT.[33] This sight was shown publicly in 2013, but has usually been proposed as an upgrade to the T-62M, replacing the old 1K13 image intensifier integrated night sight, laser rangefinder, and missile guidance block. The 1PN-96MT was not adopted by the VSRF since it was judged inferior to the *Sosna*-U (lower view range, lower resolution, no automatic target tracking, and no independent two-plane stabilisation), but it is likely that *Sosna*-U production cannot keep up with the need to replace the horrendous losses suffered, so the 1PN-96MT is now being used as a substitute.[34] The official designation of this variant (if it exists) is unknown.

Protection

Russian T-72B3Ms during exercises, featuring the 'removable modular protection kit'. The side hull fabric ERA bags have been mostly abandoned now in favour of more sturdy metal boxes similar to the turret ones. (Sputnik)

The original T-72B3 had virtually the same protection as a late 1980s T-72B with *Kontakt*-5 ERA. The only real difference was that the *Luna* IR searchlight was removed, allowing for slightly greater turret coverage. However, there were still significant gaps left in the turret ERA protection. On the T-72B3M, newer *Relikt* ERA replaced the side *Kontakt*-5 armour protection, as well as longer side-skirts. It is not known why the frontal hull and turret retained *Kontakt*-5; it may be due to *Relikt* being heavier than *Kontakt*-5.[35] Some slat armour can also be added on the hull sides to protect the engine and around the rear of the turret, as the *Relikt* did not extend that far back on the pre-war models.

This protection can be supplemented by a 'removable modular protection kit' consisting of welded metal containers with *Kontakt*-5's 4S22 ERA elements, attached to the turret sides, and fabric containers with 4S22 elements separated by inserts, attached by straps to the hull side. This kit is not related to the *Relikt* ERA. Its primary purpose is to provide added protection against shaped charge weapons in urban environments. There are a total of nine containers on the turret sides and 24 on the hull sides for the T-72B3's kit, with a total of 90 and 204 ERA elements, respectively.[36] The fabric hull containers have proven to be fairly fragile, and more recently metal containers were adopted instead.

With combat experience, T-72B3s produced since the 2022 invasion have received extended *Relikt* side panels to cover the entire hull side. Older *Kontakt*-1 blocks are also used to cover as many gaps in the original ERA scheme as possible, including the gun mantlet and the lower glacis of the hull; why they used the older *Kontakt*-1 instead of *Kontakt*-5 or *Relikt* is anyone's guess. Netting has been placed around the turret front in order to presumably catch and deflect RPGs that might otherwise hit the exposed turret ring and deflect them into the ERA. Of note as well is the additional modular protection containers mounted on the turret rear, taking the place of the OPVT river-fording system that is a standard fixture on Soviet and Russian tanks. This suggests that the Russians probably do not intend to do any fording with these tanks any time soon, especially after the disastrous attempt at Bilohorivka in May 2022.

The Nagorno–Karabakh War in 2021 between Armenia and Azerbaijan saw the widespread use of uncrewed aerial systems (UAS), or colloquially 'drones', particularly the Turkish TB-2 Bayraktar with light guided bombs. In light of this experience, the VSRF adopted roof slat armour for its tanks and issued instructions on how to prepare these devices to the troops. This slat armour (also known pejoratively as a 'cope cage' in pro-Ukraine online circles) was also claimed by some to help protect against the Javelin ATGM, which dives down on its target in top-attack mode. The effectiveness of this armour is questionable, though a definitive answer would require a detailed scientific study comparing losses: Ukrainian tests using the Javelin suggest that it is ineffective, and combat experience seems to confirm this.[37]

During the early stages of the Russian invasion, the roof slat armour was a common fixture on Russian T-72B3s, and also seen on other Russian tanks including T-90As, older T-72s, and even T-62s. However, it has not been as commonly seen after the early stages of the war. Some Russian tankers have complained about the added weight, reduced visibility, and additional difficulty it causes when evacuating the tank, and they likely do not view the questionable added protection to be worth these drawbacks.[38] There are, of course, differing opinions that view the cage armour more positively.[39]

'Mobilisation' T-72B3s of the Western Military District somewhere in occupied Ukraine, March 2023. The upper one has *Sosna*-U, while the lower one has 1PN96MT and no crosswind sensor. The additional protection is now mounted in metal containers on the hull and turret. (Mil.ru)

T-72B3Ms at the Kadamovsky training grounds in Rostov-on-Don in January 2022, preparing for the invasion of Ukraine the next month. These feature the standardised roof slat armour, but not the additional protection kit. (Mil.ru)

Mobility

T-72B3 catches some air during one of those 'flying tank' displays the Russians are so fond of. (RIA)

Automotively, the T-72B3 is almost identical to the T-72B. As on the T-90, the old 840hp V-84 was found to be underpowered due to the increased weight (46.5 tonnes), thus the T-72B3M received the new V-92S2F engine. Developing 1,130hp, this gives a power/weight ratio of ~24hp/t, better than on the T-90A and not that far off from the power/weight ratio of a T-80 (~27hp/t). The transmission has also been modernised into an automatic one, though it retains the same speeds. This significantly eases the driver's workload compared to the old manual BKP transmissions. He also has a modern digital engine management display system and a rear-view camera.[40] It is unknown if all of these upgrades have been retained on the mobilisation T-72B3. The dual-pin tracks of the T-90A have also been adopted to replace the old unsatisfactory single-pin tracks.

These modernisations still do not address some of the T-72's fundamental mobility flaws, however. The reverse speed is still the atrocious 4km/h, and the dual-pin tracks do not appear to really help with the mud problem: on 11 February 2022, less than two weeks before the invasion, footage emerged of over a dozen Russian T-72B3s in the Rostov region being dug out of mud with the help of a civilian excavator during exercises, having gotten bogged down.[41] So much for the words of Russian military analyst Konstantin Sivkov, who spoke only a few days after the footage emerged, on 15 February: 'Our tanks are much better suited for advancing on muddy terrain. There is nothing to worry about, a thaw can only stop Western tanks'.[42]

This T-72B3M No. 717 of the 1st Guards Tank Regiment, 2nd Guards Motor Rifle Division, was abandoned after its convoy was ambushed by Ukrainian forces near Perevolochna, Pryluky in February 2022. It moved off the road but became bogged down in the mud. (Warspotting)

This T-72B3 of the 6th Guards Tank Brigade based in Mulino, Russia was captured by the Ukrainian 51st Mechanised Brigade near Ilovaisk in August 2014. It was used for a short while before the Ukrainians abandoned it during the withdrawal from Ilovaisk. It was recaptured by Russian forces in September, and appeared in a Rossiya 1 TV broadcast, where they claimed it was an 'upgraded NATO tank' but in their ignorance showed incontrovertible evidence that VSRF units were involved in the Donbas War. (Rossiya 1)

The T-72B3 is a very good example of Russian and Soviet thinking, which prioritises improving the firepower of their tanks: the first things improved on the original T-72B3 were the modified autoloader and 1A40-4 FCS. On paper, the T-72B3s have roughly similar capabilities to the T-90A, and particularly benefit from the *Sosna*-U, which gives them far superior fire control capabilities to the original primitive T-72B. They are also substantially better than almost all Ukrainian tanks in terms of fire control, even the modernised ones. Once more funding was available, the protection and mobility were also upgraded on the T-72B3M. It particularly benefits from having a better power/weight ratio than Ukrainian T-64BVs or the BM *Bulat*.

However, they are still T-72s at the end of the day; the fundamental design has not changed, for better or worse. They also still lack many modern features that would be taken for granted on modern Western MBTs; the commander's equipment is virtually unchanged, and his situational awareness is poor by today's standards. They also do not have an SNS or a BMS; only the radio has been upgraded to the R-168 *Akveduk*. This reflects a general lack of such equipment in the VSRF, who have been known to rely on 40-year-old Soviet-era maps of Ukraine or civilian global positioning system receivers during the 2022 invasion.[43 44]

The wartime T-72B3 upgrade does not really address any of these fundamental issues either, and is a downgrade in some senses. Whether the additional protective measures taken for the T-72B3 in light of combat experience will make a significant difference remains to be seen. If the Russians continue to badly mishandle their tanks tactically, it is unlikely that any sensible amount of additional ERA is going to have a big effect on their tanks' survivability or effectiveness. In return, they lose one of the most valuable features of the T-72B3, the *Sosna*-U.

At the start of the war, the T-72B3s were by far the most numerous 'modern' (i.e. built or upgraded after 2000) tanks in Russian service: 518 T-72B3 and 465 T-72B3M tanks were in service in September 2021.[45] As such, they have borne the brunt of the fighting in Ukraine and suffered appropriately, with roughly half of the 2021 number visually confirmed to be lost by March 2023. However, the Russians are attempting to replace these losses with the 'mobilisation' T-72B3s, some economies being made to the design either to expedite production or possibly because components like the *Sosna*-U are just not sufficiently available.

There are likely still a considerable number of Russian T-72Bs in storage that can be salvaged and upgraded, although reports of '10,000 T-72s ready to be mobilised' can only be described as a fantasy. With the delays, high costs, and purported development troubles associated with the *Armata* future ground combat platform and low production of the T-90M, it is highly likely that the T-72B3 will remain the primary Russian MBT deployed to the war in Ukraine in some form for the foreseeable future.

The ZSU has captured at least 186 T-72B3s and has pressed some of these into service with their own tank units. Ukrainian tankers such as SR have noted the superiority of the *Sosna*-U thermal sight over the Ukrainian TPN-1-TPV, although he is more critical of other aspects of the tank such as its ergonomics and the T-72B3 suspension's poor performance in mud.[46] It is not known how successful Ukrainian T-72B3s have been.

Despite reports (some might call wishful thinking) to the contrary, UVZ is continuing to upgrade T-72s, though whether they can keep pace with Russian losses is another matter entirely. (UVZ)

2.3: T-80BVM: The Emperor's New Clothes

T-80BVM seen during the 2020 Victory Day Parade in Red Square, Moscow. Note the *Sosna*-U gunner sight and smaller PDT-7151 backup sight next to it. The 1G42 originally used by T-80BVs has been removed and the hole welded over. (Mil.ru)

Despite the decision to adopt the T-72/90 family as the primary Russian MBTs, some units retained T-80s, including older T-80BVs. Of course, by the 2000s it was clear that the T-80BV was obsolete as an MBT, but it still had some advantages over the T-72/90 family, particularly the gas turbine's ability to start quickly in extremely cold weather. It was felt that it would be useful to keep them around for certain units such as the 200th Independent Motor Rifle Brigade, which is based near the Arctic Circle around Murmansk, or those based in Siberia, and efforts have been made to upgrade them, culminating in the T-80BVM.

The first upgrade programme for the T-80BV was the T-80UE-1, which first appeared in 2005: essentially a marriage of the T-80BV hull with the turret of the T-80UD, which was being retired from Russian service due to a lack of spare parts that had to be imported from independent Ukraine. The engine was replaced with the T-80U's GTD-1250, and *Kontakt*-5 replaced the hull *Kontakt*-1, effectively turning it into T-80U. The original prototype T-80UE-1 used the *Buran*-M image intensifier sight with the PL-1-01 IR pulse laser, but this was replaced by the Belarusian *Plisa* thermal sight, itself a development of the *Essa* used on the T-90A and also based around the French Catherine-FC thermal camera.[47] At least 10 were known to have been built between 2007–2008, but the exact total number is unknown; the T-80UE-1 does not appear to have been built in large numbers, and for whatever reason, the Russians did not pursue the T-80UE-1 as a fleetwide upgrade for the T-80BVs.[48] The only unit known to use them is the 4GTD, which uses them alongside its T-80Us.

Instead, they have chosen the T-80BVM, which entered service in 2017. The T-80BVM shares some features with the T-72B3, with its primary improvements being the use of *Relikt* ERA and the *Sosna*-U thermal sight. The history of the T-80BVM has many parallels to the T-72B3's: in 2006, Spetsmash had begun a comprehensive modernisation programme for the T-80BV along the lines of the T-72B *Rogatka*, known as '*Motobol*'. The resulting T-80BM (Object 219M) had even more advanced features than the T-72B *Rogatka*, but the Russian GABTU cancelled the programme in 2008 after one prototype had been built. Despite repeated proposals from Spetsmash, it would be nearly a decade before the modernisation of the Russian T-80BV fleet would begin, and even then many of the advanced features of the T-80BM were dropped on the T-80BVM.

There is less detailed information about the T-80BVM available than for the T-72B3, but it does not appear to have had as many variants as the T-72B3. Since the start of the war, upgraded T-80BVs have been spotted using the 1PN-96MT thermal sight instead of the *Sosna*-U, likely for the same reasons it has begun appearing on wartime upgraded T-72Bs, as well as Kontakt-1 ERA to cover gaps in *Relikt*'s coverage. These do not have a known official designation, so they will simply be known as 'mobilisation T-80BVMs' in this book.

This T-80UE-1 was abandoned by 4GTD during their withdrawal from Trostianets, Sumy in March 2022. Note the remote-controlled AAMG mounting and commander cupola of the T-80UD's turret and the *Plisa* gunner thermal sight. (Warspotting)

Firepower

In terms of firepower, the T-80BVM is on the same level as the T-72B3. It uses the modernised 2A46M-4 seen on the T-80U, and the *Sosna*-U thermal sight and integrated FCS with automatic target tracking and integrated laser rangefinder and ballistic computer. This made the standard 1G42 sight on the T-80BV redundant, hence it was removed from the T-80BVM and the hole covered by armour plating. The obsolete *Kobra* GLATGM complex was also removed in favour of the more modern *Refleks* missile, which can be guided using the *Sosna*-U's laser. The modified MZ autoloader can accommodate modern long-rod APFSDS ammunition, inherited from the T-80UE-1. In general, the modifications to the MZ are simpler than those for the AZ on the T-90A, T-72BA, and T-72B3.[49]

If the *Sosna*-U is inoperable for any reason, there is a backup sight next to it called the PDT-7151. This is a far less capable electro-optical sight with much less view range that also lacks independent two-plane stabilisation due its mechanical linkage with the main gun. Its function is similar to the TPD-K1 sight, with the reticle adjusting for elevation based on range data and selected projectile ballistics. The image from the sight is projected onto a screen, and range-finding is done manually using the stadia markings displayed on the screen, since it does not have its own laser rangefinder.

The T-80BVM commander's equipment, as on the T-72B3, is more or less unmodified from the original T-80BV, except for a duplicate feed for the *Sosna*-U. The T-80BVM thus has the same manually operated commander's cupola, AAMG mount, and *Kristall*-PA sight, and therefore inherits all the weaknesses of the T-80BV when it comes to the commander's situational awareness. He also still has the manually operated *Utyos* AAMG.

As with the T-72B3, in light of wartime expediencies, 'mobilisation' T-80BVMs have been seen with the inferior 1PN-96MT thermal sight instead of the *Sosna*-U. While it has a laser rangefinder, it is not capable of guiding GLATGMs. Hence, the 'mobilisation' T-80BVM also has the T-80U/90's 1G46 sight, preserving the capability. These 'mobilisation' T-80BVMs would therefore at least have better fire control than 'mobilisation' T-72B3s.[50]

'Mobilisation' T-80BVM with the 1PN96MT thermal sight and 1G46 gunner primary sight. (Mil.ru)

Protection

The base armour protection of the T-80BVM is identical to that of the T-80BV from 1985. The main difference is the replacement of the *Kontakt*-1 ERA with *Relikt*: unlike the T-72B3, which uses *Relikt* only on the hull side panels, the T-80BVM has *Relikt* on the hull upper glacis and frontal turret as well. This is probably because the base armour protection of the T-80BV is substantially worse than that of the T-72B, hence it was felt that *Relikt* would be needed to give it a similar level of protection to the T-72B with *Kontakt*-5.

The hull *Relikt* array consists of 12 panels on the upper glacis and 12 more on each side of the tank. The turret array consists of 20 trapezoidal panels, leaving fewer gaps than the T-72B3's turret *Kontakt*-5 array. It is not known exactly how many 4S23 ERA elements are contained inside the panels. These are complemented by slat armour around the engine compartment sides and rear, as well as the turret rear.

The T-80BVM can also be equipped with a removable modular protection kit very similar to the T-72B3M's. It uses the same metal turret ERA containers and fabric side hull ERA containers: the only significant difference is in the number of containers, 10 on the T-80BVM's turret and 26 on the hull sides with a total of 322 4S22 ERA elements.[51]

After combat experience from the war, T-80BVMs were modified in a similar way to the T-72B3s, with extra *Relikt* side panels covering the entire side of the hull, and netting around the turret front, as well as the additional metal ERA containers on the hull side and turret rear seen on the 'mobilisation' T-72B3s.

T-80BVM No. 739 of 200MRB in Ukrainian service shortly following her capture, with the fabric bagged side hull additional protection kit. (Warspotting)

Similar to T-72B3s, Russian T-80BVMs have switched to steel containers for the additional protection kit ERA. (RT)

Mobility

The T-80BVM uses the more powerful 1,250hp GTD-1250 gas turbine engine of the T-80U instead of the GTD-1000TF, due to the tank's mass increasing to 46 tonnes, which gives a power/weight ratio of ~27hp/t. Presumably, the suspension has been reinforced in order to sustain the added weight as well, but there are no specific details known. Unfortunately, the T-80BVM still does not have an APU (unlike the T-80U and the prototype T-80BM), thus the GTD-1250 still has to be left on when the T-80BVM is idling or in combat positions. It has an improved engine management system with a 'parking mode' in order to improve fuel efficiency during such situations.[52]

In most other mobility aspects, the T-80BVM remains more or less unchanged from the T-80BV. The large rubber-rimmed road wheels, outdated manual BKP transmission, and rubber-padded tracks have been carried over. It therefore inherits the same characteristics, as well as the associated benefits and flaws, of those components.

T-80BVM at Omsktransmash without side *Relikt* ERA protection. (NGS55.ru)

Context

During the Cold War, the T-80B/BV could claim to have substantial advantages over the T-72A/B, especially in terms of tactical mobility and fire control. This is no longer true when comparing the T-80BVM and T-72B3M: both use the same *Sosna*-U thermal viewer/FCS and the mobility margin of superiority has been significantly eroded by the T-72B3M's more powerful engine, though the T-80BVM still has a slight edge in power/weight ratio. For almost all other characteristics, there is little to choose between the T-80BVM and T-72B3M. Many of the same advantages and weaknesses of the T-72B3 apply just as much to the T-80BVM, such as its fire control superiority over most Ukrainian tanks and the lack of an SNS and BMS. The only real advantage the T-80BVM has over the T-72B3M is that the gas turbine engine will start faster in cold weather. Whether that is really worth setting up and maintaining a completely different logistics chain to support the T-80BVMs used by the relatively few Russian tank units in the Arctic and Siberia is an open question.

The VSRF was known to have at least 71 T-80BVMs in service in September 2021.[53] At least 67 T-80BVMs have been visually confirmed lost in Ukraine as of February 2023, almost the entire 2021 T-80BVM fleet. This is not surprising when one sees that Russian units known to use the T-80BVM before the war include the 200th Independent Motor Rifle Brigade, 423rd Motor Rifle Regiment (4GTD, 1GTA), and 64th Independent Guards Motor Rifle Brigade (35th Combined Arms Army). All three were heavily savaged (in the case of 200MRB, effectively destroyed) during fighting in the Sumy and Kharkiv *oblasts*, especially during the Ukrainian fall counteroffensive.

The existence of the 'mobilisation' T-80BVM suggests that the VSRF still wishes to retain the T-80 in service, at least in the short term. The reasons for this are unclear: they could range from an appreciation for the mobility advantages of the T-80BVM, the logistical difficulties of transitioning a unit from T-80s to T-72s, especially during a war, or simply a need to get as many tanks into service as possible to replace the horrendous losses suffered in 2022. As noted before, the T-80 is no longer in production, hence losses can only be replaced using stored units, and these will usually have to go through refurbishment before entering service anyway.

Ukraine has captured at least 33 T-80BVMs, the vast majority during the fighting in Sumy and Kharkiv, and uses some of these in its own units. One of them, nicknamed '*Zayka*' ('Bunny'), formerly 200 MRB's T-80BVM No. 739, has achieved some fame in service with the ZSU's 93rd 'Kholodniy Yar' Mechanised Brigade, even featuring on CNN.[54] Ukrainian T-80BVM crews have generally praised the tank for its superior *Sosna*-U FCS and its good tactical mobility.

200MRB's T-80BVM No. 736 was not as lucky as No. 739, becoming one of the first Russian casualties of the 2022 invasion on 24 February. (Warspotting)

T-80BVM *'Zayka'* of 93 Mech. She has been given Kontakt-1 ERA to replace the side *Relikt* protection, since Ukraine does not produce *Relikt*. (93 Mech.)

2.4: T-90M: Russian Breakthrough?

T-90M seen during the 2021 Victory Day Parade in Moscow. Note the laser warning receivers on the turret face. ('Tukhachevskiy', Wikimedia)

The T-90M (Object 188M) is the most advanced Russian tank to see combat in the Russo–Ukrainian War at the time of writing. It is also known as '*Proryv*-3' or simply '*Proryv*' ('Breakthrough'). So, if the T-90M is *Proryv*-3, then where are *Proryv*-1 and 2? To understand the history of the T-90M, we must return to the early 2000s, when UKBTM began developing what they called a 'unified combat module' for the T-72 aimed at the export market. This modular turret could be fitted to existing T-72 hulls with relatively little modification while significantly revamping the basic T-72's primitive fire control and almost laughable commander's situational awareness by twenty-first century standards.

The research project was codenamed '*Proryv*' and the T-72's modular turret was '*Proryv*-1'. *Proryv*-1 did not meet with any export success, but UKBTM remained undaunted, and in 2005 the project evolved into '*Proryv*-2', based on the T-90S. The *Proryv*-2 modular turret was originally designed with a modular composite armour package in order for combat damage to be easily fixed by replacing individual armour modules.[55] However, the modular armour required more metal and thus increased the weight of the turret, and it was abandoned in favour of integral composite turret armour. The new turret was first publicly demonstrated on the T-90MS *Tagil* tank in 2011 at the Russian Expo Arms in Nizhny Tagil.

While the T-90MS was aimed at the export market, UKBTM hoped that the *Proryv*-2 would be adopted domestically as well, since the modular turret could be used to upgrade T-72s and T-80s along with the T-90. As early as December 2009, a model of the T-90 upgraded with the *Proryv*-2 module was presented to the Russian Ministry of Defence (*Ministerstvo oboroni Rossiyskoy Federatsii*, MO RF) and President Vladimir Putin. However, at the time, the MO RF was more interested in the *Armata* platform and the cheaper T-72B3 as the interim MBT, and there was no interest in T-90 modernisation.

Of course, the T-14 MBT component of the *Armata*, which was originally supposed to enter service in 2015, is *still* not even close to entering serial production as of 2023. It has been plagued by development problems, particularly associated with its novel 2V12 X-engine (a type that no military has been successful at putting into service so far cf. Rolls–Royce Vulture), and cost overruns. These eventually led the MO RF to greenlight the T-90 modernisation under the *Proryv*-3 programme, and thus the first T-90Ms finally entered service in 2020, 15 years after the *Proryv*-2 project began. Of the first 30 T-90Ms contracted, 20 were converted from existing T-90As, and the remaining 10 were new-build tanks.[56]

Much of the information here is based on the T-90M's export analogue, the T-90MS, which has been pretty heavily marketed and shares many of the same internal features. However it is important to remember that the Russians may not advertise their top-of-the-line material for export, and some components may differ. Wartime production pressures may also result in some features being dropped.

Firepower

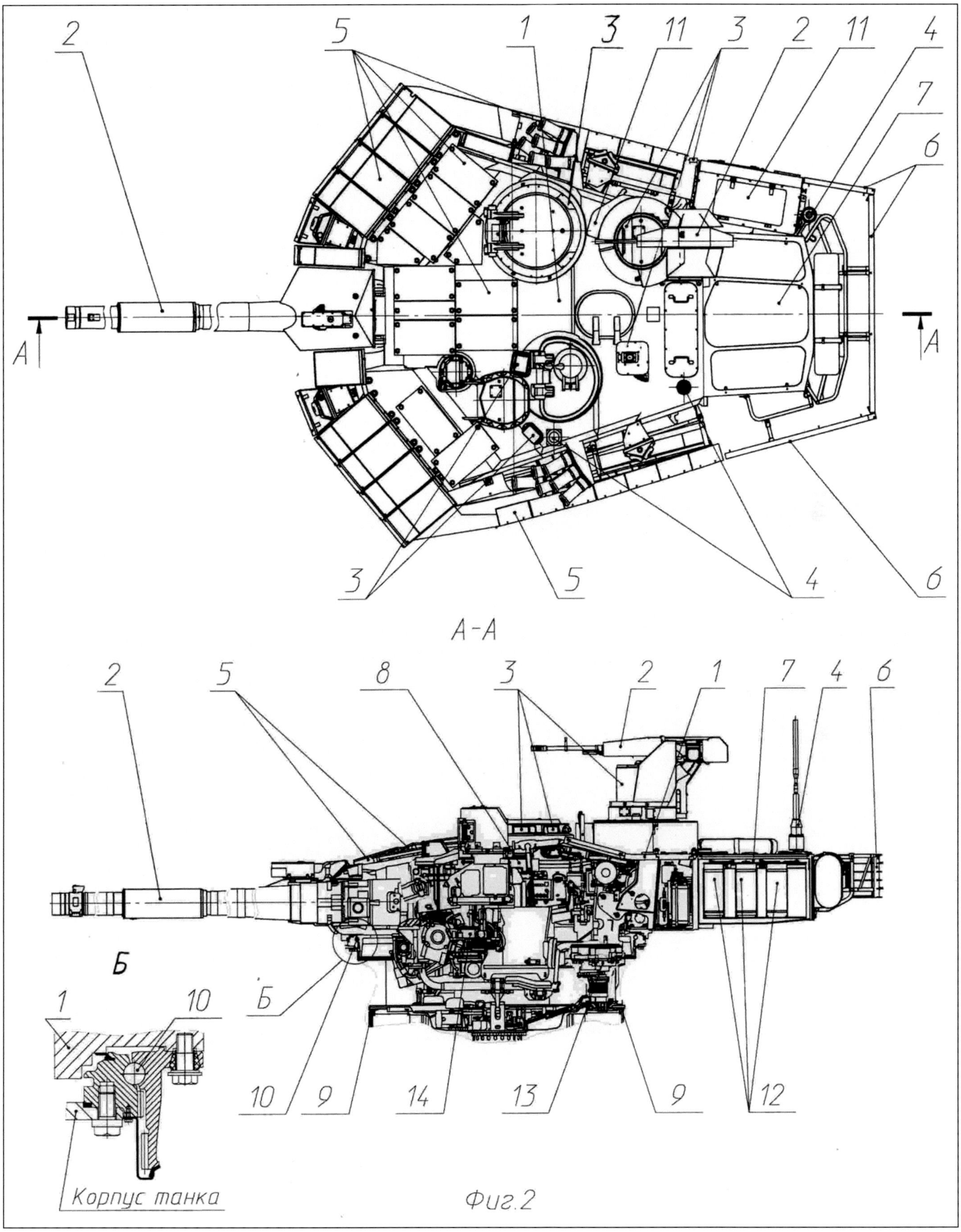

Patent drawings of the *Proryv*-3 unified combat module turret as used on the T-90M. (RU Patent 2021117325)

The main selling point behind the T-90M is its *Proryv*-3 'unified combat module' turret, patented in 2021.[57] It is armed with the same 125mm 2A46M-5 main gun as the T-90A and T-72B3. On the T-90M, it also has a muzzle reference sensor to measure barrel deformation in order for the FCS to compensate. At one point it was reported that the T-90M would receive the newer 125mm 2A82-1M of the *Armata*, but this appears to now be a pipe dream like the rest of the *Armata* programme: besides cost and production problems, the gun has a much larger breech block than the 2A46M-5 does and requires a larger autoloader carousel to fit the new rounds developed for it. Both are unlikely to fit into the T-90M without a substantial redesign. It is not known exactly what significant changes have been made to the T-90M's AZ-185-M2 autoloader.

The biggest upgrade to the T-90M's firepower comes from the new *Kalina* ('Viburnum') fire control complex. The most advanced FCS in service on any Russian tank, *Kalina* is built around the *Sosna*-U or PNM-T gunner thermal sights (the latter being an indigenous Russian design made in response to Western sanctions) and the *Sokoliniy Glaz* ('Hawkeye') panoramic CITV along with their associated sensors for ballistic calculations.[58] They are linked to a digital image processing unit, allowing for automatic target tracking, and have their own laser rangefinders and independent two-plane stabilisation, allowing the commander full control over the gunnery process if necessary.[59] The gunner also has access to the PDT-7151 as a backup if the primary sight fails. In addition to these capabilities, *Kalina* is integrated with the *Sozvezdie*-M2 BMS for greater data-sharing and situational awareness. It also incorporates the programmable munitions capabilities of the T-80UK and T-90A's *Aynet* complex.[60]

The T105BV-1 remote-controlled machine gun mount is located behind the CITV, which can be armed with either a 12.7mm (*Utyos* or *Kord*) or 7.62mm (PKTM) machine gun. Its primary purpose is to provide coverage against infantry, since it can only elevate up to 45°.[61] The T105BV-1 is aimed using the CITV and has two-plane stabilisation.[62] It can be operated by either the commander or the gunner. Eight hundred rounds are carried for a 7.62mm machine gun, or 300 for a 12.7mm. There is also a coaxial PKTM machine gun with 2,000 rounds next to the main gun.

The ammunition stowage arrangement has been altered on the T-90M as well. Besides the 22 rounds of ammunition in the AZ autoloader, the T-90M now has only eight spare rounds in the fighting compartment, located between the AZ's carousel and the engine compartment bulkhead. Another 10 rounds are located in the turret bustle in the rear of the T-90M's turret. The bustle ammunition is sealed off from the turret fighting compartment, and can only be accessed when not in combat, since the crew has to exit the tank to retrieve them. They are used to replenish the internal stowage: UKBTM originally intended to eliminate all non-carousel ammunition to reduce the risk of ammunition detonation if penetrated, but the MO RF insisted that the T-90M should have no fewer than 40 rounds.

Protection

T-90M with *Nakidka* radar/IR camouflage and *Kontakt*-1 on its lower glacis somewhere on the Zaporizhzhia front, May 2023. (RIA)

There is no public information about the base armour protection of the T-90M. However, it is safe to assume, since some of them were converted from T-90As, that the base armour protection is similar to that of the T-90A. Instead of *Kontakt*-5, the T-90M makes extensive use of the *Relikt* modular ERA, covering the upper glacis, turret front and sides, and the hull sides up to the engine compartment. The engine compartment and turret bustle are protected by slat armour. The T-90M can also be given the bagged ERA modular protection kit for the hull sides seen on the T-72B3M and T-80BVM. White aramid liners have also been installed inside the tank's fighting compartment to reduce spalling in the event of a penetration.

It is difficult to tell exactly how good the T-90M's armour + ERA is, but it is probably safe to say that it is the best protected Russian MBT currently in service. This is because its base armour is almost certainly at least as good as that of the T-90A's, while at the same time the *Relikt* ERA is not only superior to *Kontakt*-5 (at least as claimed by the developer NII Stali) but also has better coverage on the T-90M. The only other Russian tank to make as extensive a use of *Relikt* is the T-80BVM, whose base armour is substantially inferior to the T-72B and T-90's. Nevertheless, without actual test results to go by, this remains to be seen.

The T-90M's *Kalina* FCS also incorporates the laser warning receivers of the *Shtora* complex, although it does not have the characteristic IR emitters of the T-90A. As on the T-90A, the system will alert the crew when the tank is targeted by a laser designator, and it can automatically slew the turret in the direction of the laser and deploy smoke grenades to screen the tank.[63] However, this only affects laser-guided munitions, and even it has its limitations, as proven by video evidence of a T-90M being hit by a *Skif* laser beam-riding ATGM.[64]

The T-90M can also be equipped with the *Nakidka* ('Cloak') thermal and radar signature-masking fabric.[65] Based on Soviet research dating back to the 1970s, *Nakidka* consists of four layers of electrically conductive textiles and three dielectric layers in between, with an irregular-surface conductive protective sheath on top. It relies on multiple reflection and absorption of incident radio waves as they pass through the conductive layers in order to reduce the radar signature, while its temperature is closer to that of the background, masking the thermal signature. It is claimed to reduce the detection range with thermal/IR sensors by 30 percent.[66]

Mobility

T-90M without side-skirts/ERA at UVZ presented for Russian President Vladimir Putin's 70th birthday ('V.V.-70!') in October 2022. The T-90M's ancestry from the T-72 can clearly be seen in the suspension. (UVZ)

The T-90M uses the same 1,130hp V-92S2F engine as the T-72B3M. Since it is heavier than the T-72B3M (48–50 tonnes vs. 46.5 tonnes) it is safe to assume that its mobility is lower than that of the T-72B3M due to the lower power/weight ratio. It is also likely that the suspension has been reinforced to take the added weight, though there are no specific details. At least outwardly, there do not appear to be any major changes to the road wheels, tracks, or other suspension elements compared to the T-90A or T-72B3.

It is known that the T-90M uses an automatic gear shifter and engine management system, which eases driving and increases fuel efficiency.[67] However, as with the T-72B3M, it still has the same BKP transmission units, and thus the same seven forward and one reverse gears. It therefore retains the atrocious 4.2km/h reverse speed. Why UKBTM has not fixed this is unknown: the Ukrainian BM *Oplot* still uses BKP transmission units, but has been modified to give a reverse speed of 30km/h, as shall be seen later.

A rather smoky T-90M somewhere in occupied Ukraine. The *Sokoliniy Glaz* CITV and T105BV-1 remote MG mounting are clearly visible. (RIA)

It is tempting to summarise the T-90M as a T-90A with a new turret, engine, and 'shell' in the form of *Relikt*. However, this is too reductionistic: on paper at least, the T-90M has far superior capabilities in terms of fire control and situational awareness to any previous Russian or Ukrainian MBT, except maybe the BM *Oplot*. It is a dangerous opponent for any Ukrainian tank, especially since with *Relikt* it will not be easy to penetrate frontally using common weaker APFSDS rounds such as the 3BM42 or older projectiles.

Having said that, it does inherit features (and weaknesses) from the T-72 and T-90A. While the ammunition stowage has been improved compared to the T-72B or T-90A, it still retains the autoloader carousel under the turret, and there are no blow-out panels or other features separating ammunition from the crew compartment. It also still uses the same T-72 suspension, and thus will likely face the same issues encountered on the T-72. *Relikt* is over 20 years old at this point, and there are open questions as to whether it will be able to protect against modern Western 120mm ammunition once it begins arriving with the NATO MBTs promised to Ukraine.

A tank is only as good as its crew. Given the fact that the T-90M only started entering service in 2020, there has not really been much time to train crews and conduct exercises necessary when a significantly different tank type is introduced into service. This is important because the T-90M's new features are unfamiliar to existing tank crews, so they need to get experience and practice using and fighting with these new capabilities in order to be able to take full advantage of them. Crews who know how to use them will undoubtedly greatly benefit, while those who do not would be no better than if they were in a less capable T-72B3.

In September 2021, there were only 20 known T-90Ms in service with the VSRF, exclusively in the 27th Independent Motor Rifle Brigade of the 1GTA.[68] Undoubtedly, that number has increased since, given that production is underway at UVZ, and T-90Ms have been sighted in use by not only the VSRF but also by ChVK *Vagner* mercenaries.[69] Despite nominally being a 'private military company', *Vagner* was also funded, equipped, and logistically supported by the Russian government prior to their mutiny, thus it is not surprising.

Considering their superior capabilities compared to previous Russian tanks, T-90Ms have not been a decisive factor in the battles of the Russo–Ukrainian War. Indeed, the only unit known to use them prior to the invasion suffered humiliating defeats in Sumy and Kharkiv. However, there is insufficient evidence to say that the tank has been unsuccessful in service.

The ZSU is known to have captured at least two T-90Ms and pressed one of them into service with the 30th 'Knyaz Konstantin Ostrovskiy' Mechanised Brigade fighting around Bakhmut. The commander, known only as 'Yuriy', was quite complimentary of the *Kalina* FCS and its sensors, regarding it as superior to other Ukrainian tanks. However, he also said it was a 'very bad tank in terms of cross-country ability', which is not surprising at all given its T-72 roots and increased weight.[70] The Vagner mercenaries also had similar comments.[71]

On 16 March 2023, the Ukrainian Military Media Center held a public presentation titled '*Tank T-90M – "Proval" zamist "Proryvu"*' ('T-90M Tank – "Failure" instead of "Breakthrough"') presenting the Ukrainian military's findings based on a technical analysis of the other captured T-90M. In this presentation they outlined the extensive use that the T-90M makes of Western-manufactured microchips for its electronic systems, which are subject to sanctions.[72] This puts UVZ's ability to mass produce the T-90M into doubt, at least without resorting to using inferior domestically produced components.

'Yuriy' of 30 Mech. and his T-90M. Likely one of 27 Motor Rifle's tanks, it was captured with a full load of ammunition, abandoned by the Russians near Izyum when they were routed during the autumn Kharkiv counteroffensive. It is seen here with *Nakidka*. (5 kanal)

BIBLIOGRAPHY

Russian language sources are denoted by '(RU)', Ukrainian by '(UA)'.

Books

There are a fair number of books in English on Soviet and Russian tanks, but the vast majority of these are either outdated or lack much detailed or useful information.

Baryatinskiy, M., *Sovetskie tanki v boyu 1945–2008* (Yauza–Eksmo, 2008) (RU)
Baryatinskiy, M., *Main Battle Tank T-80 (Russian Armour Vol. 3)* (Hersham: Ian Allan, 2007)
Baryatinskiy, M., *Osnovnoy tank T-72. Uralskaya bronya protiv NATO* (Yauza, 2008) (RU)
Chobitok, V., Saenko, M., Tarasenko, A., and Chernyshev, V., *Osnovnoy boevoy tank T-64: 50 let v stroyu* (Yauza, 2016) (RU)
Grau, L., and Bartles, C., *The Russian Way of War* (Foreign Military Studies Office, 2016)
Grigoryan V., *Zashchita tankov* (Bauman MGTU, 2007) (RU)
Kolmakov, D. and Ustyantsev, S., *UKBTM: 75 let tagilskoy shkole tankostroeniya* (Alfa Print, 2017) (RU)
Kolmakov, D. and Ustyantsev, S., *T-72/-90. Opit sozdaniya otechestvennikh osnovnikh boevikh tankov* (UVZ, 2013) (RU)
Suvorov, S., *Tank T-90: perviy seriyniy rossiyskiy tank* (Vostochniy Gorizont, 2002) (RU)

Field Manuals

Dovidnik komandira (navidnika-operatora) tanka T-64B, MOU (2015) (UA)
Dovidnik mekhanika-vodiya tanku T-64B, MOU (2015) (UA)

Technical Manuals

For the maintenance and operation of tanks and their components, the Soviets, Russians, and Ukrainians issued technical descriptions (*tekhnicheskoe opisanie*, TO), user manuals (*instruktsiya po ekspluatatsii*, IE, or *rukovodstvo po ekspluatatsii*, RE) and military repair manuals (*rukovodstvo po voennomu/voyskovomu remontu*, RVR). Often, the TO and IE were combined into one book (TOIE). All technical manuals here are in Russian.

According to Chobitok, in Soviet times the first book (*kniga*) of a TOIE was usually secret, hence the military index (e.g. T-64A) is used, while the second book was for official use and thus the GBTU index (434) is normally used instead.

T-64

Izdelie 434 RVR, MO SSSR (1975)
T-64A TOIE kniga 1, MO SSSR (1984)
Obiekt 434 TOIE kniga 2, MO SSSR, (1986)
T-64B i T-64B1 TOIE kniga 1, MO SSSR, (1983)
Obiekt 447A (437A) TOIE kniga 2, MO SSSR, (1986)
T-64B i T-64B1 RVR (chast 1, kniga 1), MO SSSR, (1983)

T-72

Tank 'Ural' RVR, MO SSSR (1976)
T-72A TOIE kniga 2 (chast 1 & 2), MO SSSR (1989)
Obiekt 184 RVR kniga 1 (chast 1 & 2), MO SSSR (1992)
T-72B TOIE, MO RF (1995)

T-72B3

Izdelie 184 (184-1) s PNM "Sosna-U" TO, UVZ (2013)

T-80

T-80B TOIE kniga 1, MO SSSR, (1984)
Obiekt 219R TOIE kniga 2, MO SSSR, (1986)
T-80U TOIE (kniga 1 & 2), MO SSSR, (undated)

T-90

T-90S TO, UKBTM (1999)

Components

Izdelie 1A40 IE, MO SSSR (1980)
125-mm tankovie pushki 2A46M, 2A46M-1, 2A46M-4, 2A46M-5 TOIE, Zavod No. 9 (undated)
Dvigatel 5TDF TO, MO SSSR (1977)
Dvigatel V-84S IE, MO SSSR (undated)
Dvigatel V-92S2 IE, MO RF (1998)

Journals & Periodicals

Vestnik Bronetankovaya Tekhniki (VBTT) (RU)
Voprosi oboronnoy tekhniki (VOT) (RU)
Integrirovannie tekhnologii i energosberezhenie (ITE) (UA)

Online Resources

Aleksandr Dominikanets' Livejournal (LJ): dart-werther.livejournal.com (RU)
Aleksandr Dominikanets' Youtube channel (Khercrit): youtube.com/@asscold13 (RU)
Alexey Khlopotov's Gur Khan Attacks! (GKA)[†]: gurkhan.blogspot.com (RU)
Andrei Tarasenko's BTVT: btvt.info (RU)
Andrei Tarasenko's BTVT blog: btvt-info.blogspot.com (RU)
Andrei Tarasenko's LJ: andrei-bt.livejournal.com (RU)
Cate's Research-Investigation Bureau: crib-blog.blogspot.com
CAST unofficial blog: bmpd.livejournal.com
Defense Express[*]: defence-ua.com (UA)
Lost Armour: lostarmour.info (RU)
Militarnyi: mil.in.ua (UA)
Nezavisimoe voennoe obozrenie (NVO): nvo.ng.ru (RU)
Oryxspioenkop: oryxspioenkop.com
SR's YouTube channel: youtube.com/@shawshankredemption8483 (RU)
Stefan Kotsch's *Kampfpanzer im Detail*: kotsch88.de (German)
Vasiliy Chobitok's *Bronesait*: armor.kiev.ua (RU)
Vasiliy Chobitok's *Bronesait* Wiki: armor.kiev.ua/wiki (RU)
Vasiliy Chobitok's Dzen (*Tanki. Rabota nad oshibkami*): dzen.ru/media/armor (RU)
Warspot[*]: warspot.ru (RU)
Warspotting: warspotting.net

[*] Defense Express and Warspot also have English websites, but not all articles have been translated into English.

[†] Khlopotov renounced ownership of the GKA blog on 22 June 2022 after being prosecuted by the Russian government and receiving 'threats to his personal security' due to his posts criticising the war. Since then, it has apparently been run by an anonymous 'US citizen'.

ENDNOTES

Introduction

1. 'Rolled homogenous armour (RHA) equivalent' is an approximation of the effectiveness of composite or laminate armours made from different materials given as the protection offered by the given thickness of rolled homogenous armour. The interaction between penetrators and composite or laminate armours is an extraordinarily complex matter and an 'RHA equivalent' can only ever be read as a very approximate value.

Chapter 1

1. Mikhail Baryatinskiy, '*1945—2008. Sovyetskiye tanki v boyu*', (Moscow: Eksmo, 2008), p. 7
2. Baryatinskiy (2008), p. 270
3. Baryatinskiy (2008), p. 291
4. Baryatinskiy (2008), p. 345
5. The Soviet/Russian term for 'main battle tank' is '*osnovnoy boevoy tank*'. The term '*osnovnoy tank*' is also sometimes used and translated as 'standard tank' in English literature.
6. Also sometimes referred to as ZIM (*zavod imeni Malysheva*).
7. V. Chernyshev and A. Tarasenko, '*Istoriya otechestvennogo tankostroeniya (4. paradoksi otechesvennogo tankostroeniya, ch. 1)*', BTVT.
8. A. Tarasenko, '*Sovetskiy tank na poroge novoy epokhi*', WarSpot.ru (31 October 2019).
9. See A. Tarasenko, '*T-64BV v boyu*', Tarasenko's LiveJournal (20 June 2012) for more information.
10. Late production T-64As were 95 percent unified with the T-64B and used the TPD-K1 laser rangefinder-sight complex or 1A40 FCS instead of the TPD-2-49.
11. A. Tarasenko, '*20 maya 1968 g. Postanovlenie "Ob ustanovke v tank T-64 novogo bolee moshchnogo kompleksa vooruzheniya"*', Tarasenko's LiveJournal (20 May 2022).
12. N. Lukyanov, V. Lukyanov, and V. Blizgarev, '*Istoriya sozdaniya i sovershenstvovaniya tankovoy pushki D-81*', BTVT.
13. V. Chobitok, M. Saenko, A. Tarasenko, and V. Chernyshev, *Osnovnoy boevoy tank T-64: 50 let v stroyu* (Yauza, 2016), pp. 58–63
14. A. Tarasenko, '*Neizvestniy T-80U*', BTVT.
15. Lukyanov, Lukyanov, and Blizgarev, '*Istoriya D-81*', BTVT.
16. G. Rozorinov, V. Khaskin, and S. Lazarenko, '*Primenenie lazernikh tekhnologiy dlya povisheniya sroka sluzhbi izdeliya KBA-3*', Zbirnyk naukovykh prats SNUYAEtaP 3(22) (2013).
17. A. Tarasenko, '*Osnovnoy boevoy tank T-64B*', BTVT.
18. SR claims it is possible to 'adjust' the speed of the MZ's hydraulics and thus speed up loading.
19. The loading cycle is slightly longer with the GLATGM (seven seconds).
20. A. Dominikanets, '*Spravnenie T-64B i T-72B*', Dominikanets' LiveJournal (19 March 2017).
21. Chobitok et al., '*T-64*', pp. 129–131
22. Only HE-Frag and HEAT-FS projectiles are stored outside of the MZ: APFSDS and GLATGMs must be stored in the carousel.
23. A. Abramov, '*Evolyutsiya tankovikh pritselov - ot mekhanicheskikh pritselov k sistemam upravleniya ognem*', Kontenant 16(3) (2017).
24. A. Tarasenko, '*Kompleks upravlyaemogo tankovogo vooruzheniya 9K112 "Kobra"*', BTVT.
25. G. Golub, O. Dobisov, E. Zatravin, and V. Krechetov, '*Issledovanie vremni podgotovki vistrela na tankakh*', VBTT (1973)4.
26. According to Chobitok, this was because the T-64's turret had to be turned slightly to the left in order to access the driver's hatch, causing the coaxial machine gun to point over the driver. This resulted in some drivers getting shot by accident, including one fatal incident that occurred as late as 2006 at the Zhytomyr training ground. Thus, the searchlight position was changed on the later T-72 and T-80.
27. In Russian, composite armour is referred to as 'combination armour' (*kombinirovannoy broni*).
28. The Soviets and Ukrainians do not distinguish between 'proper' T-64Bs built after 1984 with the new glacis and earlier T-64Bs upgraded with the applique glacis and ERA.
29. A. Tarasenko, '*Bronirovanie sovremennikh otechestvennikh tankov*', BTVT.
30. *Ultrafarfor* is also used as a dielectric or insulator in electronics. See N. Bogoroditskiy, V. Pasinkov, and V. Tareev, '*Elektrotekhnicheskie materiali*' (3rd ed.), State Energy Institute (1976).
31. L. Ilnikova, M. Kovriga, and G. Chikalenko, *Sovershentsvovanie tekhnologi izgotovleniya bashni tanka* (VBTT, 1982)2.
32. Line-of-sight thickness of armour is the apparent thickness of armour presented to a projectile striking the target and will vary greatly according to the relative position of the firer compared to the target. As a rule of thumb, it is length of the path through the armour that a projectile would need to take in order to perforate that armour, taking into account the effects of sloping of the armour (armour sloped at 30° from the vertical will offer approximately 50 percent greater thickness than the same armour in the vertical, armour sloped at 60° from the vertical will offer approximately double the thickness compared to the vertical).
33. Tarasenko, '*Bronirovanie tankov*', BTVT.
34. A. Tarasenko, '*Balls of Soviet Tanks*', TankArchives.ca (25 April 2022).
35. Some books incorrectly claim that the ceramic spheres were replaced by aluminium filler. They are also sometimes called '*Kombination* K', a nebulous Cold War-era term for various Soviet tank composite armour types. The author has not seen it used in any Russian or Ukrainian book on the T-64.
36. Chobitok et al., '*T-64*' (2016), p. 117
37. A. Tarasenko, '*Ispitaniya NKDZ "Kontakt". Opisaniya konstruktsii i ustanovki*', BTVT.
38. A. Tarasenko, '*Ispitaniya DZ "Kontakt-1". Obstrel T-64B (T3F3)*', BTVT.
39. Chobitok et al. '*T-64*' (2016), p. 107
40. 5TDF: *5-tsilindroviy tankoviy dvigatel, forsirovanniy* — '5-cylinder tank engine, boosted'.
41. Charomsky had previously designed the ACh-30B diesel engine used on the Yermolayev Yer-2 and Petlyakov Pe-8 long-range bombers. After he retired in 1959, Leonid Golinets replaced him as chief designer for the 5TDF. See Chobitok et al. '*T-64*' (2016), pp. 15–17 and 35–39 for the 5TDF's development history.
42. This system is also used on the T-10 heavy tank, the BMP IFV series, and the PT-76 amphibious tank.
43. E. Fedorov, '*Tankoviy dizel so vstrechno dvizhuschimisya porshnyami: za i protiv*', TopWar (18 February 2022).
44. According to Chobitok, if incendiary mixtures enter the air intake, the driver must increase the engine RPM as much as possible: this allows the boosted cyclonic action to throw out the mixture particles and prevent the engine compartment from catching fire. This is impossible in a T-72 or any other tank with cassette filters. Dominikanets also confirms that the T-64 is relatively protected against Molotovs compared to the T-72.
45. S. Baranov, and V. Nikitin, '*Puti snizheniya zatrat moshchnosti v sistemakh tankovogo dizelya*', VBTT No. 2 (1985).
46. Former KhKBM engineer Yuri Apukhtin claims that under Golinets ('a passionate lover of women') work on the engine slowed down, and he was eventually removed for 'moral decay' in 1973 after Morozov strongly expressed his dissatisfaction. See Y. Apukhtin, '*Pochemu i kak poyavilis tanki T-64, T-72, i T-80. Chast 2*', TopWar (31 May 2018).
47. Suvorov relates an incident where a driver-mechanic in a neighbouring unit was told by an 'expert' to pour mustard into the 5TDF's coolant system to fix a leak from the radiator. He bought an entire pack of mustard and emptied it into the coolant system, with predictable results.

48. A. Tarasenko, *'Dvigatel 5TDF (4. Osobennosti ekspluatatsii)'*, BTVT.
49. A. Khlopotov, *'The USSR's Hungriest Tank'*, TankArchives.ca (1 March 2021).
50. A. Tarasenko, *'K voprosu o stoimosti tankovikh dvigateley'*, Tarasenko's LiveJournal (21 January 2013).
51. Uprated versions of the 5TDF (5TDFM, 5TDFMA) have been developed, but are not known to be in widespread Ukrainian use except in the BM *Bulat*.
52. Chobitok et al., *'T-64'* (2016), pp. 65–67.
53. V. Chobitok, *'T-64 (1.2.4 Transmissiya)'*, *Bronesait* Wiki.
54. V. Chobitok, *'Opisanie transmission i khodovoy chasti tanka T-64A'*, *Bronesait* (October 1999).
55. V. Chobitok, *'Vliyanie konstruktsii T-64A na ego osnovnie boevie svoystva. Podvizhnost'*, *Bronesait* (October 1999).
56. *'Izdelie 434. Rukovodstvo po voyskovomu remontu (ch. 1)'*, MO SSSR (1975), p. 326.
57. A. Tarasenko, *'Konstruktsiya khodovoy chasti tanka T-64 ch. 1'*, BTVT.
58. The Second World War Soviet KV heavy tanks had previously used similar small steel road wheels with internal rubber shock absorbers.
59. V. Chobitok, *'Khod katkov i torsioni T-64, T-72'*, Chobitok's Dzen (11 February 2023).
60. A. Tarasenko, *'Konstruktsiya khodovoy chasti tanka T-64 ch. 2'*, BTVT.
61. The torsion bars of the T-64 have a permissible shear stress of 1,500 MPa, significantly greater than the T-72 (1,300 MPa).
62. V. Chobitok, *'Azhurnie gusenitsi'*, Chobitok's Dzen (26 May 2023).
63. Simple metal track pins, like those on the early T-55 and T-62 'slack' tracks, are known as 'exposed metal joints' (*otkritiy metallicheskiy sharnir*, OMSh).
64. A. Tarasenko, *'Pro prokodimost'*, Tarasenko's LiveJournal (12 March 2022).
65. P. Kebalo, Ya. Mormilo, I. Radenko, S. Solovey, and D. Ugnenko, *'Bazoviy tip khodovoy chasti dlya perspektivnogo tanka'*, ITE (2007)3, p. 106.
66. V.F. Klimov, A.V. Istratov, and V.K. Stepanenko, *'AKT N2 ot 1 marta 1996g'*, MOU (1996).
67. SR claims that the vibrations when running on asphalt will cause the grease to leak out of the wheels and eventually lead to the internal rubber's destruction if not re-lubricated every 150–200km.
68. Tarasenko, *'Khodovoy chasti T-64 ch. 2'*, BTVT.
69. The average stiffness coefficient for the T-64 is 220kN/m vs. 265kN/m for the T-72, where a higher coefficient = greater stiffness. See Kebalo et al., *'Khodovoy chasti perspektivnogo tanka'* (2007), p. 105.
70. Klimov et al., 'AKT N2', (1996).
71. V. Chobitok, *'Spravnenie tankov T-64, T-80 i T-72 (iz lichnogo opita)'*, Chobitok's Dzen (20 January 2023).
72. Arms-Expo.ru, *'3VOF36'*. 3VOF36 is the designation for 3OF26 with 4Zh52 charge.
73. A. Sorokin, *'Sovetskaya gaubitsa D-30'*, Yauza (2018), p. 105.
74. Chobitok et al., 'T-64' (2016), p. 142.
75. D. Sobolev, *'Kak razzhimali "bronetankoviy kulak" Ukraini'*, Guildhall (9 January 2019).
76. Chobitok et al., *'T-64'* (2016), pp. 142–147.
77. S. Zgurets, *'Oruzhie Ukraini: blesk i skrezhet stali'*, Defense Express Library (2016), p. 46.
78. J. Wolski, *'T-64 na wojnie'*, Nowa Technika Wojskowa (2017)8, p. 35.
79. Defense Express, *'"Krab" ta "Bastion": nazvano stroki glibokih modernizatsiy T-64 ta "Oplotu" dlya ZSU'* (8 December 2020).
80. AUDM.org.ua, *'Staleva kinnota. Yakimi tankami voyuz ukrainska armiya'* (7 February 2021).
81. Suyi控 (@partizan_oleg), *'Ukrainian loss rate.'*, Twitter (14 February 2023).
82. CZDJournal, *'Czech defence industry companies will participate in the repair of Ukrainian combat equipment. The first contract will be the repair of T-64 tanks'* (25 April 2022).
83. A. Świerkowski, *'Czechy wyremontują ukraińskie T-64'*, Defense24 (20 February 2023).
84. Bumar.Gliwice.pl, *'Bumar-Łabędy i Ukrobronprom utworzyły centrum technologiczne napraw czołgów T-64'* (7 April 2023)
85. See I. Bazanov, *'Glavnyy konstruktor V.N. Venediktov. Zhizn, otdannaya tankam ("Otkroveniya o tanke T-64")'* (2010).
86. See Chobitok et al. *'T-64'* (2016), pp. 129–141.
87. A. Razvalov, *'Problemnie voprosi obespecheniya nadezhnosti bronetankovoy tekhniki'*, VOT (1987)6.
88. O. Georgievskiy, et al., *'Metodicheskiy podkhod k otsenke nadezhnosti bronetankovoy tekhniki'*, VBTT (1991)11.
89. The study does not distinguish between the various sub-models (T-64A/B, T-80/80B, T-72/72A).
90. See Razvalov (1987) for graph; V. Kustylkin, et al., *'Rezultati podkontrolnoy ekspluatatsii tankov'*, VOT 5(123), (1986) for data.
91. Kustylkin et al. (1986).
92. A. Tarasenko, *'Istoriya tankostroeniya SSSR. Perelomniy 1973. Chast 4'*, BTVT.info (2022).
93. Kustylkin notes that the T-80 road wheel's service life was overestimated, since they were not replaced due to a lack of spares.
94. Correspondence with Vasiliy Chobitok (2022).
95. L. Babashko, et al., *'Rezultati kontrolnikh ispitaniy torsionov seriynikh tankov'*, VBTT 1985(3).
96. According to their respective manuals, a torsion bar on the T-64 takes only one man-hour to replace. It takes four man-hours to replace a torsion bar on a T-72, due to the need to remove the road wheels on both sides of the bar to access it. Replacing a torsion key takes 4.8 and 10 man-hours for the T-64 and T-72, respectively.
97. P. Balashov, N. Zinkin, and L. Kutarev, *'Vliyanie kachestva tekhnicheskogo obsluzhivaniya na nadezhnost tankov'*, VBTT (1987)7.
98. Correspondence with Vasiliy Chobitok (2022).
99. A. Tarasenko, *'Istoriya otechestvennogo tankostroeniya v poslevoenniy period'*, BTVT.
100. In his memoirs, deputy secretary Yuri Kostenko describes a conspiracy in the finest tradition of Sir Humphrey Appleby by himself and other like-minded bureaucrats to get their preferred T-72 into production behind the back of Ustinov (Kostenko's direct superior), who preferred the T-64. He proudly describes how they waited for Ustinov and other top officials to go on vacation before altering the draft resolution on T-64 production to allow UVZ to go ahead with the T-72. See Kostenko, Yu., *'Tanki (vospominaniya i razmishleniya), chast III'*, Firma ERA (1999), pp. 90–92.
101. Lukyanov et al., *'Istoriya D-81'*, BTVT.
102. L. Kartsev, *'Vospominaniya glavnogo konstruktora tankov ("Tri Tanka")'* Militera.Lib.ru (2008). Interestingly, Dominikanets prefers the MZ escape method since it allows the driver to get into the turret at any traverse angle, even though he must first remove two cassettes. Saenko also considers it more comfortable to exit using the MZ's method than trying to squeeze through the gap above the AZ carousel.
103. The original T-72 *Ural* models carried 17 extra rounds.
104. See Chobitok et al. *'T-64'* (2016), pp. 129–131 for a description of the procedures for the AZ.
105. Chobitok et al., *'T-64'* (2016), pp. 133–134.
106. Dominikanets, *'T-64B i T-72B'*, (2017).
107. Chobitok et al., *'T-64'* (2016), pp. 131.
108. The Russians distinguish between 'tank rangefinder-sights' (*tankoviy pritsel-dalnomer*, TPD) such as the TPD-K1 and 'true' FCSs (*sistema upravleniya ognem*, SUO) such as the *Ob* and 1A40.
109. Abramov, *'Evolyutsiya tankovikh pritselov'*, (2017).
110. In his memoirs, Kartsev claims this was in order to provide an unobstructed view for the commander when firing at aircraft. See L. Kartsev, *'Vospominaniya glavnogo konstruktora tankov ("Blast peremenilas")'* Militera.Lib.ru (2008).
111. Tarasenko, *'Bronirovanie tankov'*, BTVT.
112. Early T-72s and export T-72Ms used a monolithic cast steel turret.
113. Tarasenko, *'Bronirovanie tankov'*, BTVT. Originally, UVZ was to produce the T-64's ceramic-sphere turret for the T-72, but they proved unable/unwilling to master the production process.
114. S. Ustyantsev and D. Kolmakov, *'T-72/T-90. Opit sozdaniya otechesvennikh osnovnikh boevikh tankov'*, UVZ (2013), p. 138.
115. Bazanov, *'Zhizn, otdannaya tankam ("G. A. Kheifits")'* (2010).

116. J. Warford, '*The Soviet T-72B Main Battle Tank*', Journal of Military Ordnance (12)3 (2002).
117. R. Gusev, '*Vozmozhnaya komponovochnaya skhema tanka*', VBTT (1991)12.
118. Ustyantsev and Kolmakov, '*T-72/T-90*' (2013), p. 139.
119. Tarasenko, '*Ispitaniya "Kontakt". Opisaniya konstruktsii*', BTVT.
120. A. Tarasenko, '*Osnovnoy boevoy tank T-72B*', BTVT.
121. Frustratingly, the Soviets did not distinguish between *Kontakt*-1 and *Kontakt*-V T-72Bs. The latter are often called 'T-72B *obr.* 1989 *g*.', but this is not an official designation.
122. A. Tarasenko, '*Dinamicheskaya zashchita tankov (SSSR, RF)*', BTVT.
123. R. Ogorkiewicz, '*Impenetrable Russian tank armour stands up to examination*', Jane's International Defence Review (2007), p.15.
124. Dominikanets, '*T-64B i T-72B*', (2017).
125. '*Obiekt 184. Rukovodtsvo po voyskomu remonty. Kniga 1. Chast 2*', MO SSSR (1992), p. 355.
126. Dominikanets, '*T-64B i T-72B*', (2017).
127. It is possible to use the older T-54/55/62 road wheels on a T-72, although they are slightly larger.
128. V. Chobitok, '*Khodovaya chast tankov. Podveska*', Bronesait (July 2006).
129. Klimov et al., 'AKT N2', (1996).
130. V. Kustylkin, and A. Razvalov, '*Analiz prichin otkazov pri podkontrolnoy ekspluatatsii tankov v 1975–1984 gg.*', VOT 6 (126)5 (1986).
131. Kebalo et al., '*Khodovoy chasti perspektivnogo tanka*', (2007), p. 106.
132. Klimov et al., 'AKT N2', (1996).
133. Dominikanets, '*T-64B i T-72B*', (2017).
134. SR, '*O khodovoy T-64 i T-72 (about suspension of T-64 and T-72)*', YouTube (31 March 2023).
135. Dominikanets, '*T-64B i T-72B*', (2017).
136. J. Mason, '*The Ragtag Army That Won the Battle of Kyiv and Saved Ukraine*', Wall Street Journal (20 September 2022).
137. Radio Svoboda, '*Tankovi boyi: molodi tankisty ZSU znyshuyut rosiyisku bronetekhniku*', YouTube (28 July 2022).
138. A. Khlopotov, '*Obzor sostoyaniya tankovikh voysk Vooruzhennikh Sil Rossii na 2021 god*', GKA (15 September 2021)
139. L. Angorskaya, '*Poroshenko v Chugueve po sluchayu Dnya Vooruzhennyih Sil Ukrainyi*', RedPost (6 December 2014).
140. Oryxspioenkop, '*The Kielbasa Connection: Polish Military Aid To Ukraine*' (18 August 2022).
141. M. Alginin, and 'Askai707', '*5th Tank Brigade of the Russian Army in the Battle for Debaltseve*', InformNapalm (4 March 2015).
142. The Swedish *Stridsvagn* 103 ('S-tank'), which entered service in 1967, was the first service tank to use a gas turbine, in a hybrid power plant along with a diesel engine.
143. A. Tarasenko, '*Osnovnoy boevoy tank T-80 i T-80B*', BTVT.
144. See A. Tarasenko, '*Neizvestniy T-80U*' and '*Neizvestniy T-80U. Zavodskie ispitaniya tankov i ikh rezultati*', BTVT (2023) for more information on the T-80U's development history.
145. Yu. Kostenko, '*Tanki (taktika, tekhnika, ekonomika)*', NTTs Informtekhnika Moskva (1992) p. 38.
146. A YouTube video SR posted on 9 August 2022 titled '*Obnovlenie. (updated with 2A46M4)*' showed his T-64BV armed with a replacement 2A46M-4 presumably captured from Russian forces; Ukraine does not produce or import that particular 2A46 model.
147. In Russian, an 'integrated FCS' is simply known as a 'tank FCS' (*sisteme upravleniya ognem tanka*, SUOT) to distinguish it from a normal 'FCS' (SUO).
148. It is also sometimes known by its GRAU index T01-K01.
149. Abramov, '*Evolyutsiya pritselov*', (2017).
150. S. Kotsch, '*Die Feuerleitanlage des Kampfpanzers Leopard 2*', Kotsch88.de,
151. Baryatinskiy, 'T-80' (2007), p. 67.
152. Suvorov recalls asking a designer from LKZ why they did not use the T-64A's mounting on the T-80B. The reply: 'I am in full solidarity with you, comrade senior lieutenant. But we have a comrade called the chief weapons designer; when we presented the various mountings to him, we told him which machines used them. We also presented the one you just saw [*on the T-80B*] and said that no one uses it and it is unlikely anyone will, because it is imperfect. For some reason, he chose it. In ten years we will return to what is on the T-64A, but this will be a modernisation, and people will receive Lenin Prizes'. From A. Tarasenko, '*Osnovnoy boevoy tank T-64A*', BTVT.
153. Tarasenko, '*Bronirovanie tankov*', BTVT.
154. Tarasenko, '*Ispitaniya "Kontakt". Opisaniya konstruktsii*', BTVT.
155. A. Tarasenko, '*Osnovnoy boevoy tank T-80U "Object 219AS"*', BTVT.
156. Tarasenko, '*Dinamicheskaya zashchita*', BTVT.
157. The model used was somewhat incorrect, missing the 20mm HHA plate between the cellular filler blocks.
158. A. Tarasenko, '*Sravnenie bronirovaniya Leopard 2 I, M1A2 Abrams, Leclerc, T-80U*', BTVT.
159. The Klimov factory and its design bureau have a long history of producing aero-engines. They are also responsible for the RD-33 turbofan that powers the MiG-29 and the TV3-117 turboshaft that powers nearly all Russian helicopters.
160. News.ru, '*Gde rulit prozhorlivyi tank T-80*' (15 December 2018).
161. Khlopotov, '*USSR's Hungriest Tank*' (2021).
162. Baryatinskiy, '*T-80*' (2007), p. 37.
163. Cate's Research-Investigation Bureau, '*T-80 MBT engine air filtration and dust prevention systems*' (17 May 2023).
164. Tarasenko, '*T-80 i T-80B*'.
165. '*Obiekt 184. RVR 1-2*' (1992), p. 353, 355.
166. Klimov et al., 'AKT N2' (1996).
167. Khlopotov, '*USSR's Hungriest Tank*' (2021).
168. M. Skaremyr, '*T 80U Delrapport 1.Framkomlighetsförsök*', Arméns pansarcentrum (1993).
169. It is a myth that T-64s and T-80s were assigned to 'elite' Guards tank units while T-72s were assigned to motor rifle units or non-Guards tank units; the reality is that a unit (Guards or not) generally used the tank type assigned to its district. Example: the 'elite' 4GTD is the sole T-80U unit, but in 1985 had T-72s because that was what the Moscow district was assigned at the time.
170. Oryxspioenkop, '*Russia's Wars: Listing Equipment Losses During The First Chechen War (1994-1996)*' (21 November 2022).
171. O. Oliker, '*Russia's Chechen Wars 1994–2000: Lessons from Urban Combat*', p. 35.
172. Production in Leningrad had ceased by 1990.
173. M. Zhirokhov, '*Smenit bashnyu vo chto v Kharkove prevratyat sovetskiy tank*', DS News (27 February 2019).
174. News.ru, '*Gde T-80*' (2018).
175. Official website of the President of Ukraine, '*Mtsogo tizhnya mayemo khoroshi novini z Kharkivshini dumayu kozhen gromadyanin vidchuvae gordist za nashikh voiniv – svernennya Prezidenta Ukraini*' (7 September 2022).
176. UK Ministry of Defence (@DefenceHQ), Twitter (13 September 2022).
177. Khlopotov, '*Obzor 2021*' (2021).

Chapter 2

1. V. Andreev, M. Vasets, N. Izosimov, and V. Kasyanov, '*Kriteriy otsenki konstruktivno-komponovochnogo sovershenstva osnovnogo tanka*', VBTT (1987)5.
2. E. Zaitsev, and B. Lavrischev, '*O vliyanii operativno-takticheskogo fona na pokazateli boevikh svoystv i voenno-tekhnicheskiy uroven tanka*', Proceedings of the XIV All-Russian Scientific and Practical Conference Vol. 3, St. Petersburg (2011).
3. Khlopotov, '*Obzor 2021*' (2021).
4. A. Khlopotov, '*Notes in the margins…*', GKA (2012).
5. Aleksandr Galkin, then head of the GBTU, would later say this decision was a mistake.
6. Named after Vladimir Potkin, the chief designer at UKBTM until his death in 1999.
7. It is referred to as '*izdelie 188A1 s PNM "Essa"*' in its manuals.
8. It is claimed that the modified autoloader can rotate in both directions, but Khlopotov denies this.
9. N. Dubovitskiy, and Y. Kormiltsev, '*Avtomat zaryazhaniy tankovoy pushki*', RU Patent No. 2300722 (2007).
10. A. Tarasenko, '*Modernizirovannie tanki T-80UA, T-80UE-1, T-80BA*', BTVT.
11. A. Khlopotov, '*Pritseli PELENGA*', GKA (16 October 2011).

12. *Aynet* was considered a state secret until around 2015: Khlopotov claims that he was almost imprisoned for even mentioning it in a 2012 article.
13. In fact, *Aynet* can be used with any projectile as long as it is fitted with the EDKV electronic fuse. See A. Tarasenko, '*Osnovnoy boekomplekt otechestvennikh tankov T-64/72/80/90: kumulativnie i oskolochno-fugasnie snaryadi*', BTVT.
14. O. Alekseev, and A. Makeev, '*Effektivnie sredstva borbi s tankoopasnoy zhivoy siloy protivnika v sukhoputnikh voyskakh VS*", BTVT.
15. A. Tarasenko, 'T-90 protiv Abrams', BTVT.
16. A. Tarasenko, '*Kompleksnaya zashchita bronetankovo tekhniki Ukrainskiy podkhod*', BTVT (2007).
17. A. Tarasenko, '*Kompleks optiko-elektronnogo podavleniya "Shtora-1"*', BTVT.
18. V. Murakhovskiy, '*Ekipazh tank bil slabo podgotovlen*', Gazeta.ru (1 March 2016).
19. V. Chobitok, '*Gusenitsi "Armati". Noviy vitok razvitiya ili degradatsiya?*' Chobitok's Dzen (29 August 2021).
20. Khlopotov, '*Obzor 2021*' (2021).
21. V. Kivimäki, '*Tankspotting: T-90As in the Donbass*', Bellingcat (2017).
22. CAST (@castcentre3962), '*Bronetankovaya tekhnika v konfliktakh sovremennosti*', YouTube (14 November 2018).
23. G. White, and W. McHenry, '*An Early Operational Analysis of Russian-Supplied T-90s in Syria*', Journal of Slavic Military Studies (33)1 (2020).
24. ZSU General Staff Facebook post, 16 May 2022.
25. H. Altman, '*Pentagon Gives Statement On Russian T-90 Tank Left At Truck Stop*', The War Zone (18 April 2023).
26. Defense of Ukraine (@DefenceU), Twitter (4 October 2022).
27. R. Dzhereleyko, '*Kratko o tanke — modernizirovannyy T-72BA*', TopWar (8 December 2011).
28. A. Tarasenko, '*T-72B "Rogatka"*', BTVT.
29. L. Romanov, '*Pochemu mocshnyi rossiyskiy tank T-72B2 "Rogatka" tak i ne popal v voyska?*', Vestnik Mordovii (24 May 2021).
30. There is also a special variant of the T-72B3 that appeared in 2014 during the Russian annual 'Tank Biathlon' with a CITV and the engine upgrade of the T-72B3M. Some were sent to Ukraine to participate in the war, with at least three lost.
31. This variant is often referred to as 'T-72B3 *obr.* 2016*g.*' or 'T-72B3M' or 'T-72B3 UBKh'. None of these are officially used by the VSRF, although a technical manual from UVZ refers to it as 'T-72B3M'.
32. CAST unofficial blog, '*Tanki T-72B3 s dopolnitelnoy zashchitoy primut uchastie v Parad Pobedi 9 maya 2017 goda v Moskve*' (6 April 2017).
33. Izvestiya, '*Noviy tank T-72B3 s dorabotkami: chto izmenilos - preimushchestvo pered "Leopardami" / Izvestiya*', RuTube (26 January 2023).
34. TopWar, '*Noveyshie modifikatsii rossiyskikh tankov stali poluchat bolee prostye pritsely*' (27 January 2023).
35. CAST unofficial blog, 'Tanki T-72B3' (2017).
36. M. Rozhman, N. Rakimzhanov and V. Konev, '*Komplekt sredstv modulnoy zashchiti tanka i problemi ego ispolzovaniya*', Transformation of War in the Conditions of Globalisation of the World, Omsk (23 April 2021).
37. T. Newdick, '*Ukrainian Troops Test Javelin Missile Against Russian Cage-Style Improvised Tank Armor*', The War Zone (23 December 2021).
38. S. Balchenko, '*Tankist-geroy rasskazal o spetsoperatsii i pogib: "Pobedim no legko ne budet"*', MK.ru (24 May 2022).
39. E. Lyushilin, '*Naves pomogaet dazhe pri artobstrelah rossiyskiy ekipazh rasskazal o boevoy tsennosti kozyrkov na tankakh*', TopWar (30 January 2023).
40. CAST unofficial blog, 'Tanki T-72B3' (2017).
41. D. Malyasov, '*Over a dozen Russian tanks stuck in the mud during military exercise*', Defence Blog (11 February 2022).
42. V. Isachenkov, and Y. Karmanau, '*A spring thaw may be coming, but Russia's tanks "don't fear mud"*', AP (15 February 2022).
43. Security Service of Ukraine official site, '*SBU vstanovyla shcho rosiiski komandyry vtorhlasia v Ukrainu keruiuchys kartamy z mynuloho stolittia*' (18 July 2022).
44. D. Malyasov, '*Russian pilots still use non-military navigation equipment*', Defence Blog (20 June 2022).
45. Khlopotov, '*Obzor 2021*' (2021).
46. SR, '*T-72B3 bolee podrobniy obzor. (more detailed review)*', YouTube (7 September 2022).
47. Tarasenko, '*T-80UE-1*', BTVT.
48. At least eight T-80UE-1s have been lost in Ukraine, of which the ZSU has captured seven and is known to use at least one.
49. Tarasenko, '*T-80UE-1*', BTVT.
50. E. Perov, '*Novye tanki T-80BVM dlya spetsoperatsii na pritselakh pokhozhe priskhlos ekonomit*', TopWar (24 February 2023).
51. M. Rozhman, et al., '*Komplekt modulnoy zashchiti tanka*' (2021).
52. L. Romanov, '*Sovremennaya ili ustarevshaya: kakaya modifikatsiya pushki ustanovlena na T-80BVM?*', Vestnik Mordovii (4 November 2019).
53. Khlopotov, '*Obzor 2021*' (2021).
54. CNN, '*Ukrainian soldier uses Russian tank against them*' (11 May 2022).
55. A. Khlopotov, '*T-90M — ti pomnish, kak vsyo nachinalos?*', GKA (18 February 2019).
56. CAST unofficial blog, '*Kontrakti Ministerstva oboroni Rossii na zakupku tankov T-90M i BMPT*' (16 February 2018).
57. See A. Tarasenko, '*Unifitsirovanniy boevoy modul (UKBTM)*', BTVT Blog (31 March 2022) for the patent (RU Patent No. 2021117325) describing the turret.
58. In 2012, Russia acquired a production licence for the more modern Thales Catherine XP thermal imaging camera. It is rumoured that the *Sokoliniy Glaz* uses this instead of the *Sosna-U*'s Catherine-FC.
59. A. Khlopotov, '*T-90MS "TAGIL": FCS*', GKA (24 September 2011).
60. A. Khlopotov, '*Modernizatsiya SUO rossiyskikh tankov*', GKA (20 July 2012).
61. There is a blind spot of around 44° to the rear of the mount.
62. A. Khlopotov, '*T-90MS "TAGIL": FIRE POWER*', GKA (5 October 2011).
63. A. Khlopotov, '*T-90MS "TAGIL": PROTECTION*', GKA (17 September 2011).
64. Ukraine Weapons Tracker (@UAWeapons), Twitter (14 December 2022).
65. *Nakidka* can be fitted on any tank, but has only been seen on T-90Ms during the war so far.
66. Tarasenko, '*Rogatka*', BTVT.
67. A. Khlopotov, '*T-90MS: mobility / T-90MS: podvizhnost*', GKA (29 November 2011).
68. Khlopotov, '*Obzor 2021*' (2021).
69. Defense Express, '*Wagner Mercenaries Got a T-90M to Use it as a Howitzer, Wrapped the Sight With Wire and Don't Apply Internal Comms*' (31 December 2022).
70. 5 kanal, '*Yak trofeynna zbroya dae p#zdi ru@ni pid Bakhmutom*', YouTube (29 May 2023).
71. Defense Express, '*Wagner T-90M*' (2022).
72. Ukrainian military TV, '*BRIEFING: "THE FAILED RUSSIAN T-90M MAIN BATTLE TANK"*', YouTube (16 March 2023)

ABOUT THE AUTHOR

Wen Jian Chung is a PhD student at the University of California, Irvine with a long-term interest in tank development, particularly Soviet, Russian and Ukrainian tanks. This is his first book for Helion.